TAI CHI CH

TAI CHI CHUAN

A COMPREHENSIVE TRAINING MANUAL

Sifu Raymond Rand

THE CROWOOD PRESS

First published in 2004 by
The Crowood Press Ltd
Ramsbury, Marlborough
Wiltshire SN8 2HR

www.crowood.com

British Library Cataloguing-in-Publication Data
A catalogue record for this book is available from the British Library.

ISBN 1 86126 682 0

Dedication
This book is dedicated, with heartfelt thanks and respect, to
Master Lam Kam-Chuen

Disclaimer
Please note that the author and the publisher of this book are not
responsible in any manner whatsoever for any damage or injury of any
kind that may result from practising, or applying, the techniques and/or
following the instructions described in this publication. Since the
physical activities described in this book may be too strenuous in nature
for some readers to engage in safely, it is essential that a doctor be
consulted prior to undertaking training.

Typeset by Jean Cussons Typesetting, Diss, Norfolk

Printed and bound in Great Britain by Biddles Ltd, King's Lynn

Contents

Foreword 6

About the Author 8

Introduction 9

1   Beginning Tai Chi Chuan 12

2   Elementary Level Training in Tai Chi Chuan 49

3   Intermediate Level Training in Tai Chi Chuan 91

4   Advanced Level Training in Tai Chi Chuan 118

Appendices 131

    Appendix I   Warm-Up and Stretching Exercises 131

    Appendix II   The Pa Tuan Jin 136

    Appendix III   Excerpts from the Classics 142

    Appendix IV   Supplementary Stretching Exercises 147

    Appendix V   Advice on Full-Contact Training and Equipment 154

    Appendix VI   Self-Defence and British Law 157

    Lineage 158

Index 159

Foreword

Today in the West there is a lot more information available on the subject of China's internal martial arts than there was ten years ago. Books, videos and the Internet mean that the average student can easily gain substantial amounts of background knowledge about these arts. However, in the internal martial arts knowing something intellectually does not equate in any way to real understanding. Intellectual knowledge alone cannot compare to understanding something through one's mind, body and spirit as one harmonious entity. It is perhaps not surprising then that the average ability level of internal martial arts students, both in the West and in modern China, remains poor. Much of the reason for this can be attributed to the standards and methodology of teaching. While there is no doubt that there are teachers with great ability and understanding, the proportion of those who have been able to nurture their students to also achieve a similarly high standard remains low.

I was honoured to be asked to write a foreword to this groundbreaking book because I know that not only does Sifu Raymond Rand have an understanding of Tai Chi Chuan far beyond what might be considered usual for a teacher in the West, but also (and in a sense more importantly in the context of recommending the author of an instructional text) his senior students do too. Confucius said, 'If a man cherishes his old learning, so as to continually be acquiring new, he may be the teacher of others.' Sifu Raymond Ran can therefore truly be considered a teacher of others, and he has become one of the most experienced UK nationals in both the martial and health-related aspects of Tai Chi Chuan.

Sifu Rand began his Tai Chi training in the 1970s in the relatively rare Old Yang style under the renowned Master Lam Kam-Chuen, whose lineage is one that bypasses many of the modernizing influences on Tai Chi Chaun. His teaching methodology can therefore be said to be traditional, although many may find that it seems to be progressive in that it appears more coherent and approachable than that often encountered in the more modern and familiar type of Tai Chi Chuan practice.

In this volume you will find presented, in a clear and logical order, the steps necessary to get right to the heart of Tai Chi Chuan, and to become a skilled practitioner irrespective of which style you study. Writing a book on Tai Chi Chuan that is style-independent cannot have been an easy task, given the differences that exist between the outward manifestations of the different schools. Here Sifu Rand's gift for seeing beyond the superficial and being able to clearly explain the principles behind the movements is revealed. Although the book is presented primarily as an instructional reference text, the difficult issue of exactly what it means for a movement to be called Tai Chi Chuan is, I think, revealed here as well as it has been in English.

As a student and teacher of Tai Chi Chuan's sister art, Xing Yi, I have no hesitation in recommending this work to my own students as it has great relevance to our own art. Practitioners of other internal arts such as Baguazhang will also find much of value here. I am sure that in subsequent years many internal martial artists will find this volume a valuable companion to their ongoing study under the guidance of a good teacher.

Damon Smith
Technical Director, Yokiyusan Ko
www.yokiusan.org

The author, Sifu Raymond Rand (seated), with two of his most senior students, Sifu Douglas Robertson (right) and Sifu Donald Kerr (left).

About the Author

Sifu Raymond Rand began training in the Chinese Martial Arts, most notably Tai Chi Chuan, Nei Kung and Choy Li Fut (Bak Hsing) in January 1976, with Master Lam Kam-Chuen. Prior to this he had three years experience in Ten Shin Shinyo Ryu (Ju Jitsu) and some six months in Wing Chung.

Sifu Rand started the first class at Middlesex University in June 1983 at the request of his teacher, Master Lam, and was a founder member, and the first chairman, of the Lam Tai Chi Association which started in 1982.

In 1994 Sifu Rand founded the Middlesex University Students Tai Chi Chuan Association, in recognition of the growing number of students at Middlesex University and the need for his own senior students to have a recognized platform from which to grow.

In July 2001 the Middlesex University Students Tai Chi Chuan Association became the Yongquan Tai Chi Chuan Association (www.yongquan.org). The change of name reflects the number of students now training outside Middlesex University campuses who needed a name with which they could identify.

Acknowledgements

I would like to thank my students, family and friends for their help and support in making this book possible. Particular thanks go to Graham Barlow, Sue Huntley, Dr Robert Neville and the late Mr Wu Cheng-Hai.

Photographic models: Donald Kerr, Graham Barlow, Matthew Calvert and Daniele Buccheri.

Photography by Gavin Roberts mail@gavinroberts.co.uk

Cover design by Sue Huntley.

Introduction

There are many good books written on the subject of Tai Chi Chuan. So it may be asked: Why write another? During the years I have been practising Tai Chi Chuan I have never encountered a book on the subject that both sets out the steps necessary for proficiency in the art and lays out a comprehensive training programme with which to accomplish those steps.

The practice of Tai Chi Chuan is, essentially, a practical study of complementary yet opposite forces of nature through the medium of a martial art. In essence, a study of Yin and Yang in action. Approaching the art from this, somewhat nebulous, point of view, however, would bear little fruit for most people. It is therefore necessary to break the practice down into more manageable principles and accomplish each of these in turn before it is possible to approach the practice of Tai Chi Chuan so directly.

The vast majority of books on Tai Chi Chuan focus on particular aspects of the art or on the esoteric tradition – history, philosophy, the Classics – or, in some way, combine something of the two. Some are a sort of teach-yourself-type book aimed at the beginner, with step-by-step instructions and pictures of this or that Form, accompanied by helpful hints on training. Others focus on applications of the techniques, or Push Hands and Ta Lu training, again sometimes accompanied by helpful hints, aimed at the more advanced student.

The teach-yourself type, are often only really of any use if you are already learning the presented Form from an accomplished teacher of that style. Tai Chi Chuan Forms do not lend themselves easily to this type of learning, and stylistic differences often make such a book next to useless for a student of a different teacher, let alone a different style.

Books that focus on more general aspects of Tai Chi Chuan and works on philosophy, the classics and so on, are, by and large, more useful to a wider range of students from various styles. However, such works, though they may describe the desired attributes of Tai Chi Chuan and even show how to achieve them, usually only focus on one specific area of practice [such as Push Hands technique or applications of the form] and often only a small part of that. This is a very important area; a book such as this one doesn't have the space to cover each area in the kind of detail that books on a specific practice do. The problem here is that, to make the best use of such books, a student must be at just the point in his or her training where this information is appropriate. If not, trying to learn the techniques shown could be a fruitless experience. Moreover, it is often impossible for the student to judge how far off he or she is from being ready to practise whatever is being shown.

Many books are also useful in other ways; analysis of philosophy, academic studies, historical works, translations of the Tai Chi classics and inspirational stories of the masters are of inestimable value to the serious student.

The purpose of this book is to try to provide a set of training manuals that will help a student of any style, from beginner to advanced, both in the pursuit of his or her training and in judging his or her level of attainment against some logical milestones, together with training methods for each level. It is hoped that this will help people to make better use of other training materials as well as to provide training techniques for the enhancement of learning the major stages of Tai Chi Chuan practice.

To make this book useful to as many people as possible I have not attempted a representation of any one style of Tai Chi Chuan. The background to the work, however, is primarily that of the Yang school, as this is the most widely practised form of Tai Chi Chuan and my own background. It is assumed that the reader is either learning Tai Chi Chuan from an accomplished teacher or, if he or she is just starting out, is in the process of finding one.

Although it is possible to read this book from cover to cover, and many may wish to do so, the intention is to provide a manual to be used in conjunction with your training. Whether you read the book through first or not, the best approach is to find the point in the book that reflects most accurately your current level of training and then work with it as a form of companion.

I am not a linguist – particularly, not a Chinese linguist. I have tried to use English terms throughout the book and where Chinese words are used I have tried to make it clear, in English, what I mean by those terms. Arguments over the precise definition of Chinese words and terms I leave to others, who may be more qualified in that area.

Progress is split up into four sections – Beginner, Elementary, Intermediate and Advanced. Beginner stage is the bedrock of further progress, stretching from the student's first contact with Tai Chi Chuan to the point at which a firm foundation of the Form has been reached.

The elementary level introduces the first four of a set of twelve principles, the study of which should ultimately lead to an understanding of the one principle, called simply Tai Chi, which is the root of all principles and ultimately supersedes all other considerations.

Intermediate and advanced sections continue this process, each introducing four more principles. It may be appropriate at this point to stress that it is important for the serious student to master each part of training and each principle as it arises before moving on to the next stage. It is also inadvisable for a student to alter training methods shown to them by their teacher or develop their own training methods before reaching the intermediate stage and, even then, changes or developments made by a student should be discussed and cleared with the teacher before implementation.

The structure for the Elementary, Intermediate and Advanced sections is loosely based on the structure set out by the late master Chen Man-Ching as the Heaven, Earth and Man levels of training. These were used as a basis because they are the most succinct and inclusive breakdown of the necessary elements I have yet encountered. In some cases I have altered the order in which certain principles are tackled, in accordance with my own experience. I should state, for the record, that I am not a Chen Man-Ching stylist myself.

The study of Tai Chi is, in a sense, an embracing of a Taoist outlook on life – that is to say, it soon becomes clear that the secret of Tai Chi is to move, think and act in harmony with nature, which in the Taoist sense means to live and act in harmony with one's self and the universe. The basis of progress in Tai Chi Chuan is to develop personal power through softness, conforming to the Taoist principle that 'the soft and weak ultimately overcome the hard and strong'. When this is borne in mind it becomes clear that what is needed for the most effective progress is patient application in the day-to-day training of whatever techniques the student has been instructed to practise. Whatever it is that the student is practising should be done diligently, accurately and in a calm and relaxed manner. It is the nature of Tai Chi to follow the process of change, not to lead or force the process of change. Therefore, if training is approached in a sporadic, careless or even an overenthusiastic manner poor results will occur. Too much effort or force when training is just as bad as not enough, particularly if techniques are carried out incorrectly. At best this causes the student to go round in circles, at worst it can cause physical injury or negative results. Remember 'slowly, slowly catchee monkey'.

1 Beginning Tai Chi Chuan

Chinese Terms

To understand Tai Chi Chuan a certain amount of familiarity with Chinese thought and ideas is required. There follows a short glossary of terms and concepts with a brief explanation of each term or concept.

Tai Chi and Tai Chi Chuan

The term Tai Chi is usually translated as 'Supreme Ultimate' and is a major concept in the Chinese philosophical system Taoism. The Tai Chi is represented by the interlocking fishes, often called the Yin Yang or Yin Yang symbol (see below).

The art is more properly called Tai Chi Chuan (or Taijiquan in the Pinyin dialect). Chuan means Fist or Form and is the term given to styles of boxing. Thus, translated, Tai Chi Chuan means Supreme Ultimate Boxing.

So, Tai Chi Chuan is a type of Chinese boxing. This may seem surprising to those not familiar with the art. The Form (the sequence of movements and postures that hold the techniques of the art) is usually practised slowly in most styles of Tai Chi Chuan, and most of the movements themselves may not appear to have any obvious martial application but, taught by a teacher who understands the use of Tai Chi Chuan as a martial art, it can be a devastatingly effective one.

A common misconception is that the term Tai Chi refers to health styles and Tai Chi Chuan refers to martial styles.

The Tai Chi or Yin Yang symbol.

In fact all styles of the movement are, or should be, called Tai Chi Chuan. Throughout this book we'll follow this rule; although it is purely a question of semantics, it helps to distinguish between Tai Chi, the principle, and Tai Chi Chuan, the physical art.

Yin and Yang

The literal definition is 'the shady side of a hill' (Yin) and 'the sunny side of a hill' (Yang), the implication being bright and subdued light. These things are not absolutes though. The shady side of a hill is not pitch black, as it contains some light and the sunny side of a hill is not pure brilliance and may contain some shade.

The concept displays the mutually dependent qualities of nature. Nothing exists in isolation for it is always balanced by an equal and opposite force without which it cannot exist – light and dark, male and female, soft and hard and so on. A good example of this principle is the action of pedalling a bicycle. You cannot push down on both pedals at once. As you lessen the pressure on the left side you can increase the pressure on the right. Neither can you remove one side from the equation. For the right to be full, the left must be empty. To fill the left, you must empty the right.

The idea of Yin and Yang is of great importance to the practice of Tai Chi Chuan. Ultimately the whole art is based on this, apparently, simple principle. In fact if you truly understand Yin and Yang and their relationship to one another at every level you understand all there is to understand about Tai Chi Chuan! Of course Yin and Yang, as they apply to Tai Chi Chuan, can only really be understood on a physical and intuitive level, which is why it takes many years and much hard work for most people to come to this sort of understanding. This is because Yin and Yang are not just conceptual constructs, they are representations of the basis of all the physical laws in our world. Many complex theoretical tomes have been written in an attempt to explain and justify that last statement but, like most deep philosophies, a verbal explanation is ultimately impossible. To truly understand Yin and Yang you have to become simple rather than more complex and experience the workings of the principle in action. Tai Chi Chuan is an ideal vehicle for such experience.

Chi, Jing, Jin and Li

Ancient Chinese is a somewhat 'slippery' language. That is to say that single words often have more than one meaning or meanings on different levels. In its most literal definition Chi means 'air' but it also means 'the special or especially good rice you save to give visitors'. The combination of these two definitions gives us the concept of something intrinsically good within air.

It's important to realize that the word Chi has a different meaning from the character which is part of the term Tai Chi. In this sense the Pinyin word Taijiquan is less confusing as there is an obvious difference in the terms since the Pinyin word for Chi is Qi.

The term Chi in the martial arts is used to refer to the energy intrinsic to the breath. In classical Chinese thinking this raw Chi is stored in the Tan Tien (a point midway between the navel and the pubic bone and within the body) and can be transformed by special breathing exercises to make Jing (also written as Ching) which is a refined form of Chi energy that can be used to protect the body in combat, allow more powerful strikes with less effort through its application as Jin (also written as Chin and Gin) and promote good health.

Jin is force but a particular type of force peculiar to the internal arts. It's a refined, internally generated, whole body force, as opposed to Li, also meaning force, that refers to physical, localized, muscular force. There is a saying in Tai Chi Chuan 'you can't use Li, you can't not use Li'. What this refers to is the fact that it's impossible to apply force without some physical effort and yet the type of active force that it's best to apply is not the localized, muscular kind.

Chi energy is believed to be circulated around the body via a network of meridians. Meridians are pathways around the body running just below the skin in many places and deep within the body in others. Points on the meridians are used in the practice of acupuncture to regulate the flow of Chi in order to relieve illness and discomfort. These same meridians can also be used for the process of refining Chi into Jing.

Although it is the balance of Chi in the meridians that maintains good health, without a strong supply of Chi energy an individual would appear weak and listless, even if the meridians were clear and well balanced.

Chi Kung – Nei Kung

Kung (also written Gung or Gong) means work. The term Kung Fu means 'work done well' and implies many years of training and accomplishment. You can be a Kung Fu chef, the term isn't specific to the martial arts. The Chinese term for martial arts is Wushu, though these days the term Wushu has come to mean the stylized 'athletic' martial arts practice prevalent in Communist China.

Chi Kung (also written Qigong) means 'air or intrinsic energy work' though a better term for the internal practices associated with Tai Chi Chuan is Nei Kung, which means internal work.

Tai Chi Chuan itself is, or can become, a form of Nei Kung although the term is usually reserved for a separate form of exercise that involves both moving and static postures. Even more than Tai Chi Chuan, Nei Kung requires an experienced teacher, if you wish to study it for the martial arts, as your practice must be guided by the teacher.

Taoism

Taoism is a major system of philosophical thought from China. It predates Buddhism by some 250 years and has had a direct influence on the creation of Tai Chi Chuan.

Taoism is based on a long poem attributed to a character named Lao Tzu and is, in essence, a treatise on how to live in harmony with nature and our fellow human beings by understanding the oneness of all things and the nature of the forces that give us the appearance of duality.

Confucianism, another major philosophical tradition from China, named after its founder, is based on the teachings of Taoism and of an even older work, the I-Ching.

I-Ching

The I-Ching or Book of Change is one of the oldest known written works. It dates from somewhere around 4,000 BC and was based on markings found on a tortoise shell. It is from the I-Ching that we get the concepts of Wu Chi (the void, potential or primordial energy), Tai Chi, Yin and Yang and the Tri-grams and Hexagrams often seen on Chinese works. It is also where the roots of the Five Element theory can be found (the basis for much of Chinese medicine and a source of strategy in Chinese boxing).

Although thought of these days mainly as an Oracle, like the Tarot or the Ouija Board, the I-Ching is in fact a complex philosophical system that seeks to explain the interactions between the natural forces in our world with which we all have to deal on a day-to-day basis.

The I-Ching, along with Taoism and the Five Element theory, form much of the theoretical basis for Tai Chi Chuan and while an intellectual understanding of these concepts may help a little in mastering some of Tai Chi Chuan's finer points and putting the physical practice into effect, Tai Chi Chuan cannot be learned by simply studying these concepts. It is only from living and practising Tai Chi Chuan that these things can be truly grasped and not the other way around. The I-Ching, Taoism and the Five Element theory are concepts that seek to explain the physical world or our relationship to it. That explanation is, perforce, an intellectual one while the world we live in is physical not mental, and it is only by physically embracing these ideals that we can truly understand them.

Common Questions

There are many questions a new student of Tai Chi Chuan may have, and the first lesson often produces more questions than it answers. Common among them are: 'What is this strange form of exercise?', and 'What is it designed to do?' More often than not, 'What will I get out of it?' joins the list as well. So, in line with the policy of starting from the very beginning, we'll start with the common questions that people have about Tai Chi Chuan.

Where Did Tai Chi Chuan Come From and When?

Unfortunately there is no definitive answer to this question. Depending on who you speak to, answers range from – it was created by the legendary immortal Taoist mystic Chan Seng-Feng somewhere between the tenth and twelfth centuries AD, to: an indigenous art of the Chen family, taught to a servant who went on to become its greatest exponent and change the art dramatically, in the early part of the nineteenth century. The truth may lie somewhere between the two answers.

Tai Chi Chuan as we know it today can certainly be traced to the Chen village in Henan and was undoubtedly passed from Chen Chang-Xing to Yang Lu-Chan but there is some doubt as to whether the art we call Tai Chi Chuan was indigenous to the Chen family or learned by Chen Chang-Xing from elsewhere.

Sifu Dan Docherty in his book *Complete Tai Chi Chuan* makes a detailed study of the Chen/Yang transmission, combining well-known information with unique research of his own that supports the theory that Chen Chang-Xing did indeed learn an art from outside the Chen family and passed this on to Yang Lu-Chan, rather than teaching Yang the Chen-style Tai Chi Chuan that he [Yang] then radically altered.

As to where the art that Chen Chang-Xing taught Yang came from, it is most likely that it originated in the Wu Tan mountain range amongst the Taoist hermits who have lived there for more than 2,000 years. In the past many of these hermits were ex-soldiers and also ex-bandits who would have known many martial arts styles. The Wu Tan hermits were obsessed with longevity (even with trying to obtain immortality) and quickly noticed that physical fitness, along with eating the right food and living a good lifestyle increased lifespan. It was these same hermits who developed most of the early Nei Kung and Chi Kung methods and it seems most likely that someone versed in some of the principles and practices of the Wu Tan hermits was responsible for teaching Chen Chang-Xing. Whether anyone named Chan Seng-Feng was involved in the process remains a mystery but it seems unlikely that what has become known as Tai Chi Chuan was the brainchild of any one individual but rather that it developed from many influences over many hundreds of years.

Is Tai Chi Chuan Suitable for People of All Ages?

In a word, no, although it is suitable for both sexes and for a broader spectrum of people than most martial arts. Generally speaking, Tai Chi Chuan is not suitable for young children. This is because it is slow and complicated to learn, requiring years of practice before anything really exciting starts to be possible. Indeed the Chinese generally teach external styles to children before teaching internal arts like Tai Chi Chuan.

A better bet for young children is the Japanese art of Judo. Judo is perfect for children as it gives confidence, teaches safe falling with breakfalls (which is one of the best ways to prepare for learning any martial art) and is ideal for teaching spatial awareness and the concept of correct distance.

Young children aside, Tai Chi Chuan is suitable for just about anyone else, although it is necessary to be reasonably fit and healthy, or at least to be prepared to become so, if you intend to learn Tai Chi Chuan as a martial art.

How Does Tai Chi Chuan Improve Your Health?

Tai Chi Chuan helps improve health in a number of ways. On a physical level Tai Chi Chuan is a form of gentle callisthenics. It encourages mobility of the joints and flexibility of the tendons, provides light cardiovascular work, calms the mind reducing stress and, because of the way the movements rotate (constantly shifting from Yin to Yang and back again) and combine with the breathing, provides a massage of the body's internal organs as they are rubbed together or against muscle fibres, reducing fat on the organs and helping to keep them healthy.

Traditionally Tai Chi Chuan is said to clear and balance the body's meridians as well. If these channels become blocked or out of balance, illness and disease are more likely to find a foothold. You could say that if the meridians are blocked or out of balance the body's immune system is weakened.

Can Tai Chi Chuan Help with Any Particular Medical Problems?

Tai Chi Chuan is known to have a beneficial effect on many physical problems. Circulatory disorders, digestive problems, stress-related illnesses and musculo-skeletal conditions can all benefit from the regular practice of Tai Chi Chuan.

Arthritis is known to respond well to Tai Chi Chuan training but it must be stressed that there are two forms of arthritis, rheumatoid and osteo. Although both these conditions may improve, osteoarthritis is caused by wear and tear on the joints and is unlikely to improve a lot, whereas rheumatoid arthritis is due to an auto-immune condition and, given time, may show great improvement.

It's always advisable to see your doctor before taking up a physical activity, especially if you know you have any medical condition that may affect or be affected by your practice or if you have done little in the way of exercise for many years, and always tell your instructor about any medical problem you may have when you start a class.

How Often Will I Need to Practise?

Ideally Tai Chi Chuan should be practised every day. Traditionally the best time is first thing in the morning, and there are many sound reasons to follow this tradition. First thing in the morning you have been lying in bed for seven or eight hours and your tendons have relaxed. Stretching them when you first get up will help to prepare you for the day and increase your mobility. First thing in the morning your mind is usually clearer, because you haven't filled it with the day's problems, and the practice of Tai Chi Chuan can help to energize you, calming your mind in readiness for the day's activities.

Traditionally the Chinese see the period from dawn to midday as 'young Yang', like springtime (a time when nature is naturally growing and energetic), which makes it the perfect time to engage in any activity that develops the mind or body. Perhaps most importantly, if you practise first thing there's less chance that the events of the day will overtake you and your practice will never take place. However, if it's not possible for you to practise first thing in the morning, it's OK to practise at another time.

How long you need to dedicate to your practice really depends on what you want out of Tai Chi Chuan. If all you require is to maintain and improve your health, twenty minutes to half an hour a day is sufficient. If, on the other hand, you wish to learn Tai Chi Chuan as a martial art you

need to think in terms of an hour or two a day (perhaps morning and evening) and two or three sessions a week with your teacher and/or peers if you want to make rapid progress. There are, of course, many points in between these two extremes but basically you get out what you put in.

Can Tai Chi Chuan Be Used as a Martial Art?

Yes, although it is necessary to learn it as a combat art in order to use it in this way and it does take longer to be able to apply Tai Chi Chuan to combat situations than some more straightforward arts. The advantage, though, is that Tai Chi Chuan is far less reliant on size, strength, speed and purely physical attributes than other, more quickly learned arts.

In the modern sense of martial arts, there is a long-standing debate as to whether or not Tai Chi Chuan can be taught and used as a martial art using the Form as a template.

Hard styles have patterns as a repository of techniques, however, such a pattern cannot be applied in an ABC method, as opponents will attack with subtle differences including varying angles and degrees of speed and force that make last micro second adjustments necessary in order for the techniques to be effective.

The different styles of Tai Chi Chuan also have their Forms or patterns but the Form in Tai Chi Chuan has a subtly different use. True, there are techniques embedded in the Form, in fact every movement in most Forms has both a classical interpretation and a multitude of subtle variations of technique. However, technique, at least as far as self-defence is concerned, is not the main thing that we learn from the Form. Principles of posture, coordination, softness, centring and control are what is primarily learned from practising the

17

Form in Tai Chi Chuan. So, where does the martial skill fit in?

In combat, it is the adherence to the internal principles and the combat strategy of Tai Chi Chuan that are the fundamental skills and not the technique. The principal training ground for these skills is Push Hands (and I use the term loosely to incorporate all the related exercises) and direct practice of the application of the principles in the practice of self-defence strategy and sparring (including full-contact sparring).

Although techniques are important, once understood, they take a back seat to the governing principles. The incorporation of these governing principles allows the practitioner to continually adjust and fine-tune a response to an attack in a far more controlled manner than would be the case with an external style. It is important not to subordinate technique too soon however, as it is only through the practice of technique that sense can be made of the inner principles of Tai Chi Chuan.

There follows an account of an incident that happened to a senior student (Sifu Douglas Robertson) when he was on a trip to the Far East with his teenage son:

While visiting a market my teenage son was unduly pressured to buy from a street seller, whose behaviour was becoming more and more aggressive. I could see that my son was uncomfortable so I stepped between them and told the seller that that was enough. His attention immediately switched to me and he made as if to grab my clothing. I placed the fingers of both my hands on his shoulders and, by applying pressure with sensitivity to counteract his every change of direction and balance, I was able to disturb his balance to the point where he became unsteady, making him unable to move his arms effectively or readjust his stance. Recognising his disadvantage he calmed down and then asked if I was 'Bruce Lee'. We both began to smile and I told him I was a teacher of Tai Chi Chuan back home in England. He was intrigued as he was a student in a local Kung Fu school and was under the impression that Tai Chi Chuan was not a fighting art. In an exuberant manner he insisted that I should meet his Sifu so that I could demonstrate my skills to him. As his manner was now very friendly, and flushed with my success in our encounter, I agreed.

We met his Sifu at the appointed time but it quickly became apparent that this was not to be a totally friendly encounter! Whether something had gone awry in the translation or the Sifu felt he had something to prove I don't know but it was clear that he had come prepared to fight as if challenged! He was younger than me, a strong, flexible looking, man and appeared to be very determined. I had the distinct feeling that I was getting into deeper water than I liked but with his students around him I could find no way to back out gracefully. As we faced each other I decided that there was more riding on this than East v West or Hard v Soft, indeed it was the very credibility of Tai Chi Chuan itself, not to mention the fact that I could end up on the receiving end of a thoroughly good hiding!

I raised my guard, right hand extended in the traditional manner, in preparation. My opponent slipped into a low strong stance and brought his right wrist up hard against mine and I knew immediately that I had him! As I felt the force of his arm on mine I yielded to it, keeping contact but slipping round so that I could seize the inside of his wrist. Not meeting the resistance he had expected had the effect of uprooting him slightly and I twisted my body and sank my weight, applying Jin to his arm. He was lifted off his feet and fell heavily on the base of his spine and before he had a chance to recover I locked his arm and pinned him to the floor, whereupon he instantly cried stop.

When the encounter was over the Sifu became very friendly, much to my relief, and, through our interpreter, asked many questions about where I had learned such effective Tai Chi Chuan. He seemed particularly impressed by the speed of his downfall, the fight having lasted just a few seconds.

This victory was given to me by the application of the higher principles of Tai Chi Chuan, applied instinctively and automatically under great pressure (indeed, the 'technique' used would be hard to find in any classical interpretation of the movements of the Form). It was the result of many years of practice coupled with trusting those principles in my moment of need.

The above account has been included, in the student's own words, in order to convey something of the unique nature of Tai Chi Chuan when used as a fighting art.

Finding a Teacher

As with any worthwhile activity the first steps are often the most important, as the path taken at the outset will usually dictate the destination as well as the journey.

The first thing a prospective student needs is a teacher. This may seem like stating the obvious but some thought should be given by the would-be student as to what he or she wants out of Tai Chi Chuan before embarking on many years of study. Such soul searching is particularly necessary when starting Tai Chi Chuan because of the diversity of emphasis between styles and teachers.

There are five major styles of Tai Chi Chuan: Chen, Yang, Wu, Sun and Hao (sometimes called Little Wu). Within these major styles there are myriad stylistic differences even between different schools within the same lineage. Some place more emphasis on health, some on aesthetics and contemplation and others on the martial aspects of the art.

If you only wish to study Tai Chi Chuan for health any competent teacher of any style will be fine, though it may be better to steer clear of teachers who place most of their teaching emphasis on the martial arts aspects of the style in which case you'll be learning difficult and demanding things that you have no need for.

A person who wishes to enter style competition that is, as may be expected, dominated by the Chinese Peoples Republic as far as judging criteria is concerned at least, would be better off learning a mainstream version from one of the main styles, that is, Yang, Chen, Wu, Sun or Hao, or the recently created 'combined Form' (that, as the name implies, seeks to combine elements of the five main styles into one Form), from a teacher versed in the stylized approach of the mainland Chinese Wushu system, if he or she is to have much success.

If you wish to learn Tai Chi Chuan as a martial art you need to find a teacher versed in all aspects of Tai Chi Chuan, who can demonstrate and apply the martial principles and techniques under combat conditions.

What to Look for in a Teacher
It is not my intention to imply any bias regarding which style you should choose, indeed choice is often limited by availability, but where a choice of teacher does

exist the above factors should be borne in mind (that is, what do you wish to accomplish in your study of Tai Chi Chuan).

Having decided what you want to achieve, the next step is to find an instructor who is competent in the most suitable style available. Checking an instructor's competence can be very difficult for a beginner. If the selected teacher is endorsed by a reputable association, such as the TCUGB (Tai Chi Union for Great Britain), BCCMA (British Council for Chinese Martial Arts) or other MAC (Martial Arts Commission) or Sports Council affiliated organization, this should go some way to ensuring their reputability. It is by no means a foolproof guarantee, however, any more than not belonging to such an organization is proof that the person is not competent. So how do you select a teacher having decided on what you want out of the art? There is no definitive answer to this rhetorical question, there are far too many variables, but the points laid out below should go some way in helping to make a decision:

1. An instructor of Tai Chi Chuan who is teaching classes run by him or herself, not merely helping their own teacher in the instruction of a class, should have a minimum of three years' practice behind them and, unless they have ten or more years' experience, they should still be training regularly with their own teacher. It is difficult to imagine anyone with less experience being competent to teach such a demanding subject.
2. A teacher should be able to name his or her instructor and trace the lineage of the style being taught back to a recognized teacher in one of the major styles (that is, Yang, Chen, Wu, Sun or Hao [Little Wu]).

3. A teacher of ten or more years' experience will usually be able to perform the Long Form associated with his or her style, not just a modern or abridged Form. Although not important for most people, if you want to learn the origins of the art it's important to know the source from which the abridged version came.
4. A teacher of Chinese origin who learned Tai Chi Chuan in Hong Kong will very likely be a member of the Chinese Wu Shu Association Ltd, that publishes a book, a kind of who's who in the martial arts, and a reference in this publication may be considered a good guide to authenticity.
5. A teacher who was taught by a Chinese Sifu may well have been given a letter of introduction or recommendation (the traditional method for a teacher to certify a student) by his or her teacher or he or she may hold a certificate issued by an association. Either way, the document should bear the teacher's name and that of his or her teacher.

Generally speaking, a teacher who complies with one or more of these criteria may be considered competent to teach Tai Chi Chuan within the framework of his or her style.

If you wish to study Tai Chi Chuan from a martial arts point of view or to enter competition, whether Push Hands, stylistic or combat, you must find out a little more.

If you wish to enter competition you should check to see if the proposed teacher has a history of competition wins, either for themselves or for their students, in the type of competition that you wish to enter.

If Tai Chi Chuan is to be studied in its entirety, including its use as a martial art, the intended teacher should be able to demonstrate the techniques of Tai Chi Chuan in a convincing manner and be able to show prowess in Push Hands (a training method used in Tai Chi Chuan). Most reputable teachers, if approached respectfully, and questioned about the style they teach will be happy to advise the prospective student about where to train, even if this is with someone else.

Finally, it is advisable, if at all possible, to observe what the prospective teacher's senior students can do and how they behave and so on. After three or four years' training, students should show a depth of understanding, some proficiency in Push Hands and at least a grasp of the classical techniques of Tai Chi Chuan. After seven or more years' training, students should be able to show competence in the application of Tai Chi Chuan technique and be able to generate the required intrinsic energy to make those techniques work. All students, in a properly run class, should be well behaved and courteous and a cheerful and harmonious atmosphere should accompany training sessions, even in martially orientated classes.

These points are made because there are classes where, although the teacher is well accomplished, the expertise does not seem to find its way to the students, even after some considerable time training. It is true that not all students, even those who remain with a class for many years, are capable of or wish to acquire great skill but it should be expected that at least some are capable and have the desire to plumb the depths of Tai Chi Chuan.

There may be several reasons for the above. Not everyone who wants to teach is cut out to be a teacher, no matter how proficient at Tai Chi Chuan they may be. Some teachers, for reasons known only to themselves, are averse to revealing the higher skills of Tai Chi Chuan to some or all of their students. Traditionally, the Chinese have a system of 'indoor' and 'outdoor' students. Some Chinese teachers, and even some Western ones, hold a ceremony known as Bai Shi to mark the acceptance of an individual to indoor training, though others simply invite the student to private training sessions. The indoor students are treated as part of the family and are privy to all the teachings; the outdoor are seen as 'apprentice' students and are not admitted to the higher aspects of Tai Chi Chuan. The usual reason given for this is that it allows the teacher to weed out those who are not suitable for the higher skills. However, Tai Chi Chuan is such a sophisticated art that it is largely self-secret, in that, people with a bad attitude or who wish to learn to fight for the wrong reasons can rarely tolerate the many years of training it takes to learn anything really powerful and if they can they will most probably find themselves transformed by the training into someone worthy of the art after all.

It is said that there is no such thing as a bad student, only bad teachers. While there may be exceptions that prove the rule, this statement is true much of the time.

NB Some teachers maintain the, again traditional, Chinese practice of accepting students by interview, another way to gauge the character and motivation of students prior to spending many years teaching them. Don't forget that teachers have an investment of time and energy in the students they teach as much as the students have an investment in their learning.

Starting Out

Having found a teacher, the next step is to establish a positive training pattern. No doubt your instructor will set some ancillary exercises and training techniques but some explanation as to how and why these should be done may be helpful.

In general, exercises fall into three categories in Tai Chi Chuan:

1. Stretching or Warm-Up Exercises

The purpose of these is twofold: firstly to increase the student's flexibility by stretching the tendons, and muscles in order to improve performance of the postures in the Form; secondly to provide a warm-up/cool-down routine so that the student does not pull muscles and tendons while training.

It is important, therefore, that both these exercises are performed every day (usually first thing in the morning, as this proves to be the most effective time to increase flexibility) and whenever the Form is practised. Many variations of these exercises exist (a small selection is provided in Appendix I). It is not necessary, however, to perform very many of them at any one time, a suitable warm-up for Tai Chi Chuan can be achieved with six to ten exercises.

The main groups of joints and muscles that need to be worked on are: the ankles, knees, hips, waist and lower back, together with calves, thighs, hamstrings and inner thigh tendons. The rest of the body – namely the upper back, shoulders, arms and neck – need some work of course and any competent teacher will tailor-make exercise sets according to an individual student's needs by adding to them, changing or augmenting them as training progresses or the need arises.

2. Health/Circulation Exercises

Again there are many of these, like the eighteen wonderful exercises, the Pa Tuan Jin and so on, and they are all facets of the Chi Kung.

The Pa Tuan Jin is a particularly good system based around eight major exercises, with many variations to suit individual needs and health requirements, all done in sets of eight. The most common set of exercises appears in Appendix II. This type of exercise must be done daily but it's not necessary to include them in your warm-up every time you practise the Form. Their purpose is primarily to encourage Chi (intrinsic energy) to flow smoothly around the meridians (channels in the body, used in acupuncture, that act as pathways for Chi energy), they are also very relaxing and gently align the body's organs and in some cases the skeleton.

3. The Nei Kung/Chi Kung

Chi Kung literally means energy training, Nei Kung means internal training. There are many forms of this exercise also, some with specific functions such as 'Iron shirt' Chi Kung, that is designed to build up the body's strength from within so that by the time the effect reaches the surface the practitioner is able to withstand large forces directed against him or her without ill effect. Such training must also be done each day but again there is no need to include it in the warm-up exercises. A particularly good system is 'Zhan Zhuang' (pronounced 'Jam Jong') Chi Kung, taught by Master Lam Kam-Chuen.

Chi Kung/Nei Kung is a subject in its own right and is best taught one-to-one in any case, so there are no examples in the Appendices. However, Master Lam has produced an excellent book called *The Way of Energy*, published by Gaia Press, if you are interested in Zhan Zhuang Chi Kung.

Chi Kung exercises are internally directed. That is to say they are as much an exercise of the mind and spirit as of the body and are designed to promote the build-up of Chi within the body, train the awareness and encourage the transformation of Chi to Jing, which refers in this context to internal or refined intrinsic energy, that can be applied to attacking techniques, defensive techniques, or to cushion the body from an unavoidable impact.

A few words of caution: it is generally best to avoid books on the Chi Kung/Nei Kung that go into detail about the experiences that you are likely to have or describe the experience of the author, unless they have been specially recommended by a competent teacher, preferably your own. This is for two reasons; firstly, because of the diversity within the Chi Kung a student may start off on a track that is inappropriate to their own system or inappropriate to their level of training; and secondly, because, taught properly, a teacher of Chi Kung needs to give continuous advice and guidance that can only be given at the appropriate time, judged by the student's own experiences in the form of feedback. This is so that a student does not imagine experiences in their practice because they have heard or read about them before training. It is also vitally important that a student of the Chi Kung is practising circulation exercises, of the type mentioned above, and practises the Chi Kung diligently and accurately.

The key to all training techniques in Tai Chi Chuan from stretching exercises to the Nei Kung and the practice of the Form itself are: regularity, accuracy and the correct amount of effort. It is far more beneficial to practise a small amount, in the correct manner, every day than to practise for long sessions sporadically.

In the early stages of training a good tip is to be gentle with yourself. If you set

A group practising standing Chi Kung.

yourself long training regimes or a goal of many rounds of the Form, it is odds-on that you will not keep up the training for many months, let alone years. It is far better to have a realistic daily workout suited to your enthusiasm, lifestyle and stamina and to gradually increase your workout because you enjoy the training and feel comfortable with it, than to start off in an over-zealous manner (perhaps because someone says you should or that they spend heroic amounts of time training and you feel the need to keep up), then flag and feel guilty that you have not met your own targets.

The important thing is to train a little *every day*. Working on the things or parts of the body that are weak, repeating exercises as accurately as possible (always check with your instructor if you are unsure as to whether you are performing correctly and watch him/her and your senior fellow students closely in order to check your movements) and work within the limits of your own body.

In the practice of Tai Chi Chuan it is as important not to overdo things as it is not to underdo them. When stretching, for instance, you should increase the movement until the muscles and tendons feel well stretched, but stop at the first signs of pain, then simply hold the position and relax and never bounce on the area you are stretching. Practising this way will gradually and naturally increase the range of movement.

Don't forget: Tai Chi Chuan seeks to welcome and embrace change not to push or force change. It has its roots in Taoist philosophy that teaches the virtue of harmonizing yourself with nature, not trying to get nature to harmonize with you.

Learning the Form

As previously stated, the intention of this book is not to give a step-by-step guide to any particular Form, but rather a guide to training any Form and some basic points that are fundamental to all styles of Tai Chi Chuan.

The same general advice, given in the last chapter with regard to exercising, is also true when practising the Form. (That is, it is important to train regularly, using an adequate, though not overambitious programme of training, and above all to practise as correctly as possible.)

Correctness
Correctness, of postures, stepping, and direction, is the main ingredient of early training. If the Form is learned accurately in the beginning it will save much time later on when you reach a more advanced level. It is important to remember, however that most teachers of Tai Chi Chuan will teach a simplified version of the Form at first and gradually refine the movement over time.

Due to stylistic differences it is not possible to advise on small details of your Form, these must be gleaned by closely observing your teacher and senior fellow students. The following points are, however, universal to all styles of Tai Chi Chuan:

Breathing
In the early stages of training no attempt should be made to align the breathing with the movement. This is because breathing in Tai Chi Chuan is very subtle and powerful and the movements are slow and complex. Until the Form can be practised smoothly, continuously and correctly, trying to cope with correcting the postures and coordinating the breath with the movement will prove far too taxing. Also, if done incorrectly, the pressure in the abdomen on the internal organs, during an incorrect movement, could conceivably cause injury or negative effects. At this level, you should breathe naturally and abdominally, that is to say using the lower abdominal muscles to operate the diaphragm, by directing the breath to the Tan Tien. This allows the chest and upper abdomen to remain relaxed and causes the air to circulate to the bottom of the lungs (NB When the air is drawn into the lungs by the lower abdomen, even a relaxed breath will circulate more air than a powerful thoracic breath). During all practice the mouth should be kept closed, all breathing should be done through the nose, and the tongue should be placed on the upper palate just behind the front teeth. This is because two meridians, known as the Functional and Governor (or Ren and Du) meridians, meet at this spot, one at the tip of the tongue and one on the upper palate. Therefore, by keeping the tongue on the point, it is as if a switch is closed allowing

Chi to flow around these meridians more effectively.

Posture

Although posture does vary a little from style to style there are some fundamental rules that apply to all styles. These are the posture requirements of Tai Chi Chuan. In fact only ten of these rules can be said to directly relate to posture and at this stage the five listed below are enough to be going on with:

1. **Suspending the head:** when standing still before commencing the Form, with the legs straight but not locked at the knee, you should feel as if you are suspended by a thread attached to the crown of the head (the point from which medical training skeletons are hung). You can pull up gently on your hair at this point to get the right feeling. This will ensure that your back is straight, your head properly aligned, and give a light feeling to your body. Once achieved, this aspect should be maintained throughout the Form and returned to if you move your head (to check the position of your feet for example).

2. **Rounding of the shoulders:** when practising Tai Chi Chuan it is important that the shoulders, and upper body generally, are almost completely relaxed. Therefore, in this context, the Western idea of good posture (shoulders back, chin up, chest out) is no good at all.[1] A good way of achieving the correct position is to take one very deep breath, filling the lungs up to the top, then release that breath quickly through the mouth, relaxing at the same time. This has the effect of relaxing the chest and at the same time rounding and relaxing the shoulders.

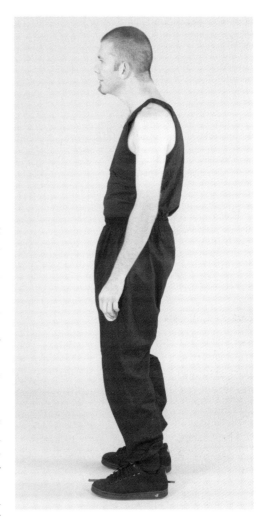

A common, slouching posture.

3. **Rounding of the knees:** once the Form has commenced, your knees should be rounded at all times. There are few exceptions to this in any style of Tai Chi Chuan, though there are one or two. It is most important, however, that whichever of your legs is carrying the majority of the weight of your body is rounded at the knee. Correct rounding of the knee requires that an imaginary vertical line from the knee joint going

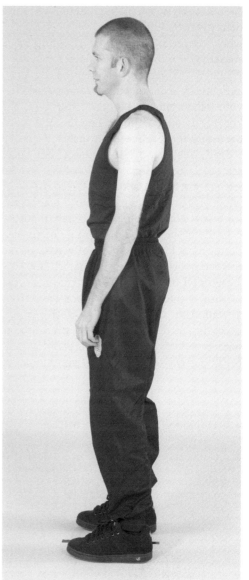

Western 'military' type posture.

Correctly balanced posture.

straight down to the floor would run straight through the ball of the foot in a front stance. To help you judge this: you should be able to see the inside crescent and tip of your leading big toe when you look down. If you can see most of your foot your weight is too far back and you are double weighted (a concept that will be covered later on), if you cannot see your toe at all, your weight is too far forward and you are in danger of injuring your knee.

A common error with beginners is the tendency to straighten the supporting leg when executing a kick or standing in a stance where the feet are almost together. Allowing the legs to straighten also causes stepping to become irregular and stiff. If you follow the rule about rounding the knees this should never happen and your balance will benefit enormously.

Last, but by no means least, there is a martial arts saying: 'Don't offer broken leg'. If you fail to keep the knees rounded when fighting they present an ideal target for a low kick, designed to break or dislocate the knee joint. This is most often evident on back stances. A good way to prove this point yourself is to take a piece of straight wood and a piece of curved wood of similar thickness, prop them up against a wall, the curved one with the curve towards you, and attempt to break them with a side kick. The straight stick will break easily (unless it's very green wood),

breaking the curved piece will be much more difficult, both because a curve is a stronger shape and because it will tend to twist out of the way.

4. **Centring the coccyx:** the coccyx is the small group of vertebrae at the very bottom of the spine. In the practice of Tai Chi Chuan, it is necessary to consciously push these small bones forward a little, in order to align the hips and create a dead straight line from the crown of the head through the perineum (the space between the genitals and the anus).

5. **Drooping the elbows:** in order for the arm to be relaxed yet physiologically strong in any forward thrusting movement, the elbow must always be lower than the wrist.

It will take a little effort, at first, to maintain these posture considerations

Knee too far forward in front stance, incorrect.

Knee too far back in front stance, incorrect.

Knee correctly positioned in front stance.

TOP LEFT: Incorrect back stance with front leg straight.

ABOVE: Correct back stance with front knee rounded.

The straight leg leaves no room to escape a low side kick.

The rounded front leg allows room for manoeuvre.

throughout your practice of the Form but it is necessary for the acquisition of a good foundation in the movement.

Direction

It says in the Tai Chi classics 'if the body is in error then the fault will be found in the legs and feet'. The first, and simplest, meaning of this statement is that the feet must be set down in the correct direction at each step. If this is not the case, then the next step will be difficult and uncomfortable to achieve or, more probably, will be thrown further out of position and so on

until your Form is in complete disarray. As a general rule the leading foot is always pointing in the direction in which the torso is heading and usually in the same direction as the leading hand, though there are some exceptions. Again it is important to watch your teacher and senior fellow students closely to correct the orientation of your own Form.

Slowness

Always relax and take your time when practising any aspect of Tai Chi Chuan. There is little point in running through the

Brush Knee, body correctly aligned in vertical posture.

system that involves teaching the whole Form step by step in a simplified manner (sometimes called a square Form), leaving just long enough for the student to grasp the basics of one posture before moving on to the next one. This method means that the whole Form can be completed in a much shorter time than with the old method, is more interesting to learn and more palatable to the majority of modern practitioners. It does mean, however, that many people practise the series of movements that make up the Form without ever practising the individual postures and joining movements, and therefore end up with a superficial knowledge of the Form.

Ultimately Tai Chi Chuan is not a series of separate, or even connected, postures but one long movement from beginning to

Brush Knee, incorrect posture, bad alignment.

Form on 'remote' as it were. Tai Chi Chuan is an art that requires conscious practice if training is to yield improvements and not merely go round in circles. Remember: if your training doesn't eradicate bad habits, or you practise inattentively you will probably be doing more harm than good to your Form.

Breaking the Movement Down

The traditional way to teach Tai Chi Chuan was to show one movement or posture and leave the student to practise it (giving occasional advice and correction) until it was nearly perfect. This method of teaching has given way to the modern

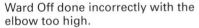

Ward Off done incorrectly with the elbow too high.

Ward Off done correctly with the elbow drooped.

end, though it is not possible, or even advisable, for a beginner to try to practise this way. In fact it's better to break each movement down as much as necessary into two, three, or even four components, pausing briefly between each one to check for correctness of the posture considerations mentioned above, position and alignment of the feet, continued relaxation, and alignment of the arms and hands. Practising this way will also help

you to get a rein on your mind that, at this stage, is often flustered and in such a hurry that there sometimes seems to be no time to get things right even when you are moving slowly. It is similar to the experience of learning to drive a car – to begin with there seems to be no time to change gear, check the mirror, look where you're going and steer. Once you are proficient, however, there is plenty of time to do all these things and hold a conversation with a passenger at the same time (though it is always necessary to look where you're going).

The factors mentioned above are the main ones to concentrate on when you begin learning the Form. Though, of course, as you progress further in the art many other considerations need to be taken into account.

The most important thing to remember is to constantly check your movement – both against what you understand the correct way to perform it to be and against your teacher's and senior fellow student's movement. Never be afraid to ask if you're unsure as to whether or not you are doing it right.

NB When you lower your head to check positioning, don't forget to lift it back up to the correct position before continuing. Otherwise you will end up with a posture that leans forward due to looking at the floor.

Training Tips for Beginners

It perhaps goes without saying that regularity in training is the most important thing to acquire in Tai Chi Chuan, especially as it was pointed out twice already. There are a number of additional things to bear in mind, however, if you are to get the most out of your training. The first thing to decide is what it is you want to achieve in Tai Chi Chuan. This will depend largely on why you wanted to practise the art in the first place, so it helps to ask yourself what brought you to Tai Chi Chuan. If you are interested in the martial arts[2] you will be demanding more of yourself physically and in terms of time spent training than, for instance, someone who is practising because they want to be more healthy and to pursue Tai Chi Chuan as a gentle form of exercise. Likewise, someone who has a particular health problem and has sought out Tai Chi Chuan as an aid to recovery, may have to start out carefully and gradually increase their training as they become stronger.

Even if you are unclear about why you are practising Tai Chi Chuan or are interested in it from an aesthetic or artistic point of view, the keys to productive practice are regularity and the application of conscious action. That is to say, training with all your faculties engaged. It's so easy, once you have established a training pattern, to do it on automatic, convincing yourself that it's OK because you're doing half an hour a day, even if you don't really remember doing it half the time. Some martial arts, and some sports, can be practised this way with reasonable success but not Tai Chi Chuan. It's better to do ten minutes' conscious training than an hour of unconscious movement, so it's important to have a good idea of what you need to work on and why.

One of the great things about Tai Chi Chuan is the fact that it takes many years of patient application to achieve anything worthwhile. This may seem at first like a disadvantage but it all depends on your point of view. Tai Chi Chuan allows enormous scope for self-development. So, although it's helpful to have an idea of what you want to achieve at the outset, don't be surprised if your sights have shifted once or twice before you're done.

Tai Chi Chuan for Health

If you are practising Tai Chi Chuan because you have been unwell or have an intractable condition, such as arthritis, back problems, hypertension and so on, you should do two things before beginning training. Firstly, check with your doctor to make sure it is safe for you to practise Tai Chi Chuan. If necessary, discuss your condition with your prospective teacher to get an idea of what training he/she would recommend and then discuss the proposals with your doctor to ensure their suitability. Secondly, pay the greatest attention to what your teacher tells you and be sure to practise what you are shown both accurately and in the way you were told to practise it. Above all, stop training if you begin to feel any negative effects or if you become overtired and consult your teacher again.

If your motive for training is simply to be more healthy, then, provided you have no serious health problems to start with, it's a simple matter of establishing a daily pattern of training and then practising in a thoughtful manner. The best time of day to practise Tai Chi Chuan is usually reckoned to be in the early morning (as discussed in the glossary of Chinese terms). Of course there is nothing to stop you doing some more training in the evening (most respected authorities recommend combined morning and evening practice).

Traditionally, the Chinese say that early in the morning is the beginning of the Yang cycle[3] and that it is better to practise at this time because more Chi is flowing in the atmosphere, particularly in natural places, near running water and under trees.

Some people may find morning practice impractical, milkmen for instance, or unpalatable and it is perfectly acceptable to practise in the evening, if you can set a time aside regularly, rather than not practising at all. Whenever you practise, it is important to warm up properly before working on the Form and to do an adequate amount of stretching, using the techniques shown to you by your teacher, in order to increase your range of movement. It makes sense, of course, to combine your stretching and warm-up (that will probably be the same or similar exercises anyway) but don't forget to repeat them if you do decide to train again later on.

It also helps to do some stretching exercises after you finish training. This is because stretching after training helps the muscles to get rid of accumulated work toxins and also releases any stiffness you may have acquired due to incorrect practice. If you neglect to do this don't be surprised if you ache the next day or the day after that. If you also practise the Chi Kung you will need to incorporate these exercises into your training schedule but there is no need to include them in your warm-up as such.

In the morning, start with Chi Kung (if you are receiving instruction in this art) and follow with exercises and then the Form, in the evening just warm up, then practise the Form. Practice of the Chi Kung is very demanding and must be done just how it was shown to you. It's important to always do the moving exercises, such as the Eighteen Marvellous Exercises of the Chi Kung or the Pa Tuan Chin or whatever you have been shown, if you are engaged in standing posture training, such as Zhan Zhuang or Iron Shirt Chi Kung, to help balance your circulation of energy around the meridians.

Tai Chi Chuan as a Martial Art
If you are keen to study Tai Chi Chuan as a martial art, the way you train will need to go up a gear or two. Essentially, your training schedule will be much the same as that described in the paragraph above but you will need to practise for longer, probably do more, and more demanding, exercises and, above all, take a more serious approach to training. This does not mean you have to become fanatical or sombre about your practice, rather that you will need to be even more focused when training.

Stretching and Chi Kung exercises need to be practised assiduously and the correct spirit must be cultivated while practising the Form. If you have previously studied another martial art, or still practise one, you will be no stranger to routine training. If this is your first experience with learning a martial art, the advice in the previous chapter still holds true; build up your schedule gradually, and pay close attention to how you are instructed to train. It's said that all roads lead to Rome. Anyone who has been on the M25 will tell you that this is not true. Some routes go round in circles.

Warm Up and Cool Down

Just a quick word about your pre- and post-training regime. Although Tai Chi Chuan is a gentle exercise, mobility, and therefore stretching (particularly of the legs, hips and waist), is an important part of its practice. Before you start to practise the Form you should stretch your limbs, but before you stretch you should do some light aerobic work to increase the blood flow to your muscles and tendons. This light aerobic work could take the form of running on the spot, working on an exercise bike, working out lightly on a punch bag, skipping or anything that raises the heart rate and gets the body moving. Five minutes should be enough, though there is nothing to stop you doing a little more.

When you begin your stretching don't be overenthusiastic. Gradually increase the range of the movement until you reach your furthest comfortable extension, then increase the range just a little, until you can just feel it stretching, then relax. You may be able to repeat this procedure once or twice more but don't force yourself to stretch too far – not only is there a danger of injury but overstretching tends to cause the tendons to shrink back further than

they ought and can be counterproductive (two steps forward, one step back) and *never* 'bounce' while stretching as this will cause the tendons to react by stiffening up against the stretch and will reduce mobility.

NB You should wait until your breathing and heart rate have slowed to normal before practising the Form.

Training the Form

Master Lam advised a three-stage method of practice with regard to the Form itself.

The first time you practise the Form (or however much of it you know) in any session you should just do it as smoothly as you can but without too much concern. This is because the first run-through will inevitably be poor and it's best to just get it out of your system before you train proper.

During the next part of your practice you should practise the Form with an eye to improving your standard. You should run through the movement at least once but preferably as many times as you have time to spare and the energy to do it. At this stage your practice should include; pausing to correct your posture, correcting the direction of your steps, relaxing stiffness from your joints and correcting the movement itself. Try to be as diligent as you can and work hardest on the things you know to be weak. It's a good idea to have a notebook to hand so you can jot down questions on things you're uncertain about. You can then ask your teacher for advice when you next go to a class, as such questions often seem to skip your mind once you get there.

Finally, before you finish your training session, practise the Form through once as if you are already an expert. Begin confidently and run through the movements as smoothly as you can, incorporating everything you know in your movement but don't be concerned if you get some things wrong; just make a mental note of those movements or postures that don't seem quite right so you can give them more attention in your next session. This last stage helps to solidify your practice and also to reduce any stress from the previous section of training.

Single Push Hands

Once you have completed learning the movements of the Form, and spent a little time allowing them to sink in, you will probably receive your first taste of Push Hands (though some teachers begin this instruction earlier).

Push hands is most often begun at this juncture for three reasons. Firstly, most students have reached a temporary impasse with the Form and cannot take any further refinement at this stage. A period of time must elapse where you consolidate what you have just learned before attempting to develop the Form further. This doesn't mean you stop practising what you've learned but rather that you concentrate on getting what you've done so far right, as far as you understand it, before moving on. Secondly, Push Hands is an ideal method of adding deeper understanding of the movement in Tai Chi Chuan. Thirdly, Push Hands helps to develop correct posture (because it cannot be done well if your posture is poor) and also roundness, the next aspect of Tai Chi Chuan to be studied.

Push hands is the primary sparring method in Tai Chi Chuan. It is unlike most other sparring methods in the martial arts, however, in that it is done, for the most part, relatively slowly and gently, at least at this level of training.

The primary consideration in Push Hands is sensitivity. When practising you should never behave as if you are engaged in a mock battle or trying to score points over your partner. The idea is to replace mere physical attributes, such as strength, speed, quick reflexes and even cleverness, with an acquired ability to sense what your partner is about to do by following his or her movements and merging with them, yielding to the force used against you and sticking to your partner's every move so that you attain a superior position and are able to effortlessly overcome them. If you fall back on natural strength or speed or trickery to overcome your partner you will never replace these simple, natural abilities with higher skill. Master Lam used to say 'If you practise this way (incorrectly) even if you win (the session with your partner) you lose'. You lose because you are not progressing in the acquisition of skill in Push Hands, that would eventually allow you to overcome faster, stronger opponents than yourself. If you fall back on your natural abilities, such as strength or speed or cleverness, you will be lost when you have to face a stronger, faster or smarter opponent than yourself. Also, your partners will gradually acquire true skill and your innate abilities will be overcome, so you will be left behind.

It's very important to practise Push Hands with the right attitude. Think of the exercise this way: when you attempt to apply a technique on your partner, you should do so with the attitude that you are helping him or her by forcing him or her to defend. When you are forced to defend, you are being helped to improve and should be grateful to your partner. This device may help you to overcome the 'win at all costs' attitude that seems to get everyone at one stage or another and is an obstacle to further improvement.

The most common Form of Push Hands to be taught at this stage is single, fixed or one-step Push Hands. Single, because only one hand at a time is used to contact with your partner. Fixed or one-step, because once you have set your stance, either no movement of the feet is allowed (with the possible exception of the raising of the toes of the forward foot) or, only one step, forward or back, at a time is allowed. This form of Push Hands, though unrealistic in terms of combat, helps to develop the posture, flexibility and stability necessary to move on to more sophisticated practice.

Single Push Hands Format

Partner 'A' adopts a back stance, with the inside of his or her right foot approximately one fist distance from partner 'B's' right foot. Partner 'B' adopts a forward stance with his or her right arm forming the Peng (Ward Off) position (that is, as if holding a balloon clasped against the chest). Both partners place their feet one-and-a-half to two shoulder widths apart (be careful not to adopt too long a stance because although this gives good balance and trains the legs, it also tends to make movement slow and awkward).

Partner 'A' places his or her right palm on the wrist of partner 'B's' right arm. Partner 'A' pushes forward, towards the centre line of 'B's' body, while at the same time moving from a back stance to a forward stance. Partner 'B' yields to the incoming force, trying to match the amount of 'giving way' exactly to the force of the push (no more, no less), while at the same time moving from a forward stance to a back stance. Partner 'B' should try to keep the Peng shape from collapsing by moving away from the force of the push (as if a thin reed were between the palm of the right hand and the chest which 'B' does not want

to break). There will come a point where it is not possible to move back any further without being pushed off balance or collapsing the Peng position (the imaginary reed begins to bend); when this point is reached 'B' should drop the right elbow and turn the right hand palm down (deflecting) 'A's' push away from the body. In order to accomplish this, it is vital that 'B' keeps his or her back straight, sits low in the stance, drops the right hip and uses only just as much force as is needed to keep the hand in place (If the Peng position is too rigid 'B' runs the risk of being pushed back by his or her own arm). Once the push has been successfully dealt with 'B' moves to the push position and 'A' adopts the Peng position and the process is reversed.

As you can see from the above, provided both partners perform perfectly, a circular movement takes place with push and deflect alternating between partners. Of course, in practice, this never goes on for long and if one partner is more skilled he or she will easily deal with the other partner's attempts to push and will be successful in pushing much of the time. It is here that the temptation comes to use strength, speed or cunning to overcome your partner but as pointed out in the second paragraph of this chapter this is not a good way to go.

Some Things to Avoid:
1. Try not to use strength to fend your partner off. If he or she is stronger than you this simply won't work; if not, it may work, but you will be learning nothing and eventually you will come across someone stronger, and your partner will learn to overcome your strength with skill.
2. Using speed to catch your opponent unawares. This has its place later on but for now it will just cause frustration.

Speed is never a cultivated asset in itself; it's timing that really matters, but, at a certain point, it is useful to know how to deal with a sudden fast movement. Later on in your training, don't be surprised if your teacher expects you to use some fast movement. For now, speed should be avoided.

3. Using cunning to find ways to alter the situation to give yourself an advantage. A common example of this, at this level, is to push off-centre when advancing to make it difficult for your partner to defend. The problem here is that when more techniques are added, this 'advantage' suddenly leaves you open to a back-fist strike from your partner (taken from the move 'Step Up, Parry Punch' in Yang-style Tai Chi Chuan).

It is a good idea to keep your left hand (assuming you are practising on the right

Single Push Hands ready position (black shirt defending).

Black shirt yields to incoming push.

White shirt adopts Ward Off position, black shirt starts to push.

White shirt rolls back, keeping ward off position intact.

White shirt deflects incoming push.

Black shirt adopts Ward Off position, white shirt starts to push.

side) held up and covering your partner's right elbow. This is so you will be able to deal with folding techniques later on and is a habit well worth cultivating from the very beginning.

When you can perform this exercise at chest level the next step is to practise aiming for the head and groin as well, followed by shuffle-step forward, shuffle-step back, and then moving on to adding techniques such as: 'Single Whip' (where you attempt to pull your partner on as he or she pushes by taking a full step back with your right foot and pulling the pushing arm) or 'Step Up, Parry Punch' (where, having been pulled as you are attempting to push, in the manner described above, you take a long step diagonally forward with your left foot, pivot on your left foot as soon as it touches the ground, so that you are now facing your partner, and at the same time bend your right arm at the elbow, place

Single Push Hands ready position (white shirt defending).

Black shirt attempts to push off-centre to catch opponent.

White shirt deflects push out and applies back-fist counter.

your left hand on your right forearm and push your right fist towards your partner [depending on the distance it may be appropriate to kick with your right foot at the same time]).

The variations on Tai Chi Chuan technique are too numerous to mention but all rely on the same principles of sensitivity, yielding to force, and sticking close to your partner; coupled with good posture and centring.

Only by cultivating the right attitude towards the practice of Push Hands can you make progress. It is for this reason that many teachers do not encourage beginners to take part in Push Hands competition. Competition in Tai Chi Chuan has its place, but it is best left until you have sufficient experience to separate ordinary training from the training necessary for competition and have already grasped the correct method of practising Push Hands.

White shirt pushes in deep, black shirt yields.

Black shirt steps away and begins Single Whip.

White shirt neutralizes pull by following its force, stepping in.

White shirt pivots of left leg using Parry Punch and Kick.

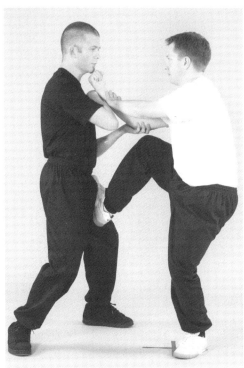

Related Practices

At some time during the beginner stage most students will be introduced to ancillary practices that may include: the Chi Kung, Push Hands, circulation health exercises [such as the Pa Tuan Chin], other sparring techniques, self-defence, breakfalls and so on. Chi Kung, Push Hands, and circulation health exercises we have already covered, so we will explore in this section some of the other related practices.

Breakfalls

It is my considered opinion that everyone who engages in a martial art, for whatever reason, should learn to breakfall (in fact I think it would be a good idea if they taught it at school as part of the National Curriculum) unless there is a medical reason why this is not a good idea, such as osteoporosis (brittle bone syndrome).

The ability to fall safely is a great asset, it has saved me from serious injury on more than one occasion, in such diverse situations as: being thrown from a horse, falling from a collapsing pair of steps, and coming off a motorbike at speed, not to mention countless, not so soft, landings when training with my teacher and my peers. Learning to breakfall should be mandatory for anyone engaged in learning Tai Chi Chuan as a martial art and I strongly recommend it to anyone wishing to practise Push Hands or any other part of a martial discipline, including self-defence.

In more than twenty years of running classes, the only serious injuries so far have been a broken wrist and a fractured collar bone, both the direct result of Push Hands training or self-defence practice by people who skimped in the practice of breakfalls. Of course, if you are old or infirm or wish to practise Tai Chi Chuan for its health aspect alone then breakfalls may not be for you. Or if all you want from the art is its meditative aspect, then perhaps you don't need to learn to breakfall. Most people find it great fun though, once the initial fear of falling has been overcome.

Some teachers of Tai Chi Chuan, and indeed of many fist-orientated martial arts, do not teach breakfalls. Usually I do not criticize the way others see fit to run their classes but on this point I make an exception. If your teacher does not teach breakfalls, I strongly recommend that you seek out the local Judo, Ju Jitsu or Aikido club and enrol for a beginners course until you are proficient in the basic breakfalls, which are: the rolling breakfall (both left and right side), back breakfall, front breakfall, side breakfall (both left and right side), and fore-flap breakfall (where the body is flipped over (possibly the result of a stomach throw or shoulder wheel) and you land first on your shoulders then on the soles of your feet, keeping the lower back off the ground).

I apologize if I have laboured this point but many are lulled into a false sense of security by the gentle nature of Tai Chi Chuan training and run the risk of unnecessary injury.

Self-Defence – Part One

It should be emphasized that self-defence techniques are dangerous and can have serious legal ramifications. Accordingly, it is essential that readers thoroughly familiarize themselves with the contents of Appendix VI (page 158) before proceeding.

The need for a separate syllabus of self-defence techniques in Tai Chi Chuan is due to the nature of Tai Chi Chuan itself. It takes a long time to become proficient in Tai Chi Chuan. It's not like more immediate styles such as Wing Chun,[4] where what you learn today you can use today. It takes some time to learn the sophisticated internal dynamics of Tai Chi Chuan and thus to make the techniques work. However, when you can make them work, Tai Chi Chuan surpasses most other fighting arts with its ability to control the combat situation through sensitivity.

The difference between self-defence techniques and the martial arts techniques that produce them is this. When you learn a martial art, you are learning to be a fighter, with the ability to defend yourself as an automatic by-product of this. When you learn self-defence you have not become a fighter. This is because self-defence techniques rely heavily on the element of surprise, which is how they can be made effective so quickly. It is also why self-defence techniques work best for women and small men. If you look like Rambo, an attacker will be expecting a tough fight, but if, on the other hand, you look like the town wimp or are a woman, most attackers will be expecting to be able to overcome you fairly easily.

Women have two extra advantages, in that, firstly, most male attackers cannot believe that they can be overcome by a woman, their ego simply will not allow it (even if the woman is larger than them); secondly, most men will rarely attempt to free fight with a woman as a first line of attack, they are far more likely to try to grab and control a woman, at least initially, and with a few carefully prepared self-defence techniques can be easily overcome. This is because when an attacker grabs you, he or she ties up one or both arms in the process and 'set-piece' escapes and counter-attacks are much more easily mastered than free-form combat. It's also much easier to use the attacker's strength against them when they exert force in the form of a grab or pull and one or both hands is locked on part of your body or clothing.

Of course, once the element of surprise is lost the whole situation changes. For this reason it must be understood that, with self-defence techniques, there is no room for half-hearted manoeuvres. Once you decide to respond physically you must act as if you are fighting for your life (which you may well be!) and give 100 per cent effort and no quarter to the attacker.

A highly trained martial artist may have the luxury of dealing mercifully with someone who has attacked them because he or she should have such vastly superior skill that it is possible to control other less highly trained people easily (even so, most experienced martial artists would tell you that 'if they were attacked the attacker must look after him or her self' and that they would take no chances). With self-defence techniques you do not have that luxury.

Once you do attempt a defence, whether successful or not, follow up immediately with aggressive palm[5] and kick combina-tions aimed at vulnerable areas, relying on the attacker's momentary loss of balance to win the day. If you fail completely at the first attempt it may be possible to feign sudden fear at your failure to overcome the attacker; then, if you bide your time and choose a good opportunity to resume your attack you may yet prevail. Remember, it is vital to follow up any successful release or counter attack immediately! Under no circumstances should you assume that your defence has been successful unless your attacker is unconscious or seriously debilitated.

Self-defence is pretty much a one-shot deal, so it must be a last resort. If there is any other option open to you then you should take it.

The use of the voice is a marvellous technique of self-defence. Often just to shout very loudly and challengingly at an attacker is enough to deter them or, in some instances, you can shout for help. It's best not to shout things like 'Help! Rape!', though, as research has shown that other people do not usually take it seriously. However, if you shout fire in a built up area, no matter how quiet the street, it's odds on that someone will take an interest (if only from morbid curiosity).

There are stories of people escaping attackers by pretending to be mentally handicapped, walking up to a stranger's house and ringing the door bell, pretend-ing to have a heart attack, pretending to have cancer, becoming friendly with the would-be attacker, asking his name and generally shaming him into retreat, delib-erately wetting themselves and simply run-ning away very fast.

It is vitally important to keep a clear head and be as calm as you can if you are attacked, so that you can spot the best course of action to take. It is also a good idea to avoid trouble if at all possible: keep away from known trouble spots, try not to walk down unlit paths at night, walk home with friends (at least in known trouble spots), don't get into taxis, cars or elevators with strangers (or even friends you don't know very well) and most importantly, try to adopt a confident (not cocky or aggressive) and friendly but aloof attitude to others.

The image you project can have a great deal to do with whether someone considers you a potential target or not. The New York Police Department once engaged the help of a woman they dubbed 'Muggable Mary'. She had been the victim of many street attacks and muggings and the NYPD set her up as bait to allow them to catch muggers in downtown New York. Studies have shown that a person's attitude and general demeanour can make them more or less of a target for street crime.

Being aware of your situation and environment is also of vital importance; not only will this help you to avoid dangerous situations and people but research has shown that many people are attacked without knowing they are in danger and a significant number of people who were aware of a potential danger were left alone once the would be attacker realized that this was the case. Attackers also like to use the element of surprise!

Self-defence techniques will vary enormously from club to club, depending on the background of the teacher. Some teachers of Tai Chi Chuan do not teach a set syllabus of self-defence techniques, preferring to teach one-off techniques as and when the occasion arises and of course some do not teach self-defence at all, preferring to leave that sort of thing to others. Good self-defence techniques should have *all* of the following characteristics:

1. Ask yourself if the technique you are practicing would work on someone six inches taller and two stone heavier than you. If the answer is no or only maybe then it's probably not a good technique.
2. Does the technique rely on you hurting the attacker, possibly through thick clothing, as the initial source of escape? If the answer is yes, refer to item 1.
3. Does the technique rely on overcoming your attacker's strength with your own? If the answer is yes, refer to item 1.
4. Good self-defence techniques should be simple to do and to remember.
5. Good self-defence techniques should not rely on intricate or flowery movements.
6. Good self-defence techniques should free you from the initial attack and stop, stun, or at least unbalance your attacker at the same time, giving you an advantage which you can capitalize on to finish your attacker and escape.

Learning self-defence techniques has to be a good idea, particularly for women and anyone in a vulnerable group. It helps to give confidence and ultimately helps in the learning of Tai Chi Chuan itself.

A word of warning for those learning self-defence techniques; don't be tempted to show off your skills to friends and family members. Self-defence techniques are often brutal and deceptively dangerous. They have to be powerful in order for a novice to make them work and they rely on the element of surprise. If you attempt to demonstrate them to your friends one of two things will be the likely result; either you'll do the technique half-heartedly in order not to injure your friend and it won't work (which may damage your confidence) or you'll do the technique properly and injure your friend (possibly losing the friend forever).

Some years ago a young lady who attended a course of self-defence classes that I was running locally, specifically for women, boasted to her brother (who was a black belt in Karate) that she had learned powerful self-defence techniques. Possibly to show how skilled he was her brother grabbed her and threw her to the floor before straddling her and placing his hands around her throat, as if he was going to strangle her. She applied a defence that she had learned in the class and (largely because he had not been expecting her to be able to do so) caught her brother by surprise, throwing him through a glass kitchen door and out into the garden! Fortunately, he was not too badly hurt and suffered only minor lacerations to the face and hands and a mild concussion but he could have been badly injured or killed!

Finally, it is all too often a 'friend' or acquaintance who is responsible for attacking women and if you demonstrate your skills indiscriminately you may be arming an attacker with the knowledge he needs to overcome you. Far better to practise your techniques only in the controlled environment of the class where you learn them.

Some further advice on self-defence and some illustrated techniques appear in the next chapter.

Touch Sparring and Tai Chi Wrestling

Not counting Push Hands or Push Hands-related exercises, such as Ta Lu (also written Da Lu) which is sometimes called Whirling Hands, there are a great number of training aids, in the form of sparring practice that are beneficial in the practice of Tai Chi Chuan. Two that are particularly useful for just about anyone, are touch sparring and Tai Chi wrestling.

Touch sparring is performed as follows: both partners place their right feet forwards and raise their right hands to touch at the wrist. The idea is to touch your partner, anywhere on the body (not counting the arms) with the right hand *only*; the left hand is used purely for defence (the right hand may be used defensively too of course). The exercise may be performed with fixed or free step and is done at speed but with no power at all, the idea being to touch your partner gently. Arms may be grasped but must be released after one second if no technique (such as a pull down or pull past) is applied and must be released at the end of that technique in any case. The whole exercise can be repeated on the left side and, when you are experienced, can be moved on to touching and defending with both hands simultaneously. This form of sparring practice is marvellous for teaching spatial awareness and is a good cardiovascular exercise.

Touch sparring ready position.

White shirt attempts a fast touch to face, black shirt deflects.

Black shirt follows hand back to touch the cheek.

White shirt attempts low touch, black shirt drops right hand to touch the body and deflects attack with his left hand.

Black shirt circles right hand round to touch the cheek again.

Tai Chi wrestling is done standing facing your partner in a shoulder-width horse stance. Each partner places his or her hands at the other's shoulders, with the arms either on the inside or the outside (or one of each). The idea is to push or pull your partner off balance while maintaining your own balance. At first no movement of the feet is allowed but as you progress, first single steps and then free stepping is allowed. The idea is similar to Push Hands in that you do not seek to

White shirt shifts his weight to the right, yielding with the right shoulder.

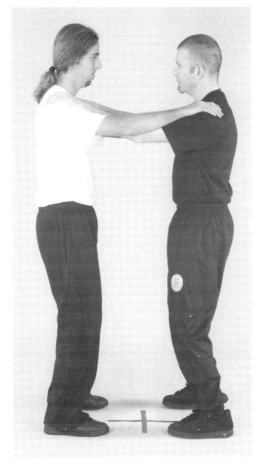

Tai Chi Wrestling, ready position, black shirt tries a push with his left hand.

dominate your partner by force alone but by applying sensitivity and yielding to your partner's force, joining with it and then overcoming it.

It's also important to realize that this is just the beginning. Learning the Form and other training techniques at this level is like learning to use the tools with which to build a house, with the actual work on the house yet to begin. The next stage is like digging the foundations and putting in the footings.

White shirt transfers power to his left shoulder, pushing black shirt off balance with his left hand.

Notes

[1] In fact this sort of posture is very bad for the body.

[2] In practice, most people who wish to pursue Tai Chi Chuan as a martial art tend to have already been involved in the martial arts (probably because it isn't always obvious that Tai Chi Chuan is a martial art to someone who hasn't been involved in them) and, if this is the case, will already have a degree of self-discipline in training and will know more about what to expect.

[3] Young Yang is from dawn to noon, Old Yang is from noon to dusk, Young Yin is from dusk to midnight and Old Yin is from midnight to dawn.

[4] A short-range flexible system of martial arts from southern China.

[5] Not punches. If you have not conditioned your hands, and they are not naturally strong, you will probably break more knuckles than teeth.

2 Elementary Level Training in Tai Chi Chuan

Having learned the basic Form of the style of Tai Chi Chuan you're practicing and allowed a period of time for it to sink in, so that you can perform the movements without hesitation in a reasonably correct manner and with the proper orientation, it is time to start work on turning these physical movements into Tai Chi Chuan.

For the movement to be truly Tai Chi Chuan it must conform to the principles of Tai Chi Chuan. The highest principle is the simplest and is represented by the Tai Chi symbol. If your Form and application is one with this it is as good as it gets. But how to achieve this somewhat abstract goal? The essence of Tai Chi Chuan is just too simple for most people to grasp in a flash of enlightened understanding, as it were. For this reason the highest principle has been reduced to twelve lesser principles. Each containing several training elements. Mastering each one in turn will eventually lead to an intuitive understanding of Tai Chi and Tai Chi Chuan.

The four principles in the Elementary stage are:

- Roundness
- Continuity or constant rate
- Slowness
- Body Lightness

and lead to the beginning of the first ability in Tai Chi Chuan; Sung Jin or Relaxed Force.

The Great Chi Debate

Before going any further in our study of Tai Chi Chuan, it's appropriate to say something about the controversial issue of Chi.

Talk to people involved in the Internal martial arts, on almost any level, and you'll quickly find yourself embroiled in a fierce debate on the existence of and practical use of Chi in the martial arts. Opinions range from those who decry the existence of something like Chi altogether, saying that the abilities of exponents of Tai Chi Chuan and other internal arts can all be entirely explained by physical phenomena, to those who insist that Chi, or more precisely Jing and Jin can be used on such sophisticated and esoteric levels that it's possible to strike or push an opponent without touching them physically. Between these two poles you'll find just about every variant of opinion, including opinions that seem to occupy both camps at once.

The problem for some people is that the existence of Chi, or Jing or Jin for that matter, cannot, at least at the moment, be scientifically proven. People can speak of their subjective experience of these forces, as in their own feelings when working the practices of the Nei Kung, or of being on the receiving end of a push or strike purported to be internally generated but there is little evidence that the feelings or the results witnessed are the result of Chi.

Feelings within the body or mind of an individual could be the result of imagination, or physiological changes brought on by intense concentration or even hyperventilation. The fact that an advanced exponent of Tai Chi Chuan can issue tremendous force with, apparently, very little physical effort could be due solely to timing, correct alignment or physical strength not immediately apparent to the witness.

In my own training with Tai Chi Chuan and the internal martial arts that at the time of writing spans a little more than 28 years, I have both experienced things within myself and witnessed demonstrations given by others that I find very difficult to explain without recourse to some other energy or something like Chi. Conversely, in all that time I have never witnessed a credible demonstration of Ling Kong Jin (the ability to strike or push people without physically touching them) and I have seen a few demonstrations by people who claimed to have this ability. Without exception, they were all either self-deluded or tricksters.

Until such time as the scientific community can conclusively prove that Chi exists or offer satisfactory alternative explanations for the phenomena associated with the internal martial arts no doubt the debate will continue, though it must be borne in mind that just because science cannot explain or test for something at the moment doesn't mean that it won't be 'discovered' and explainable in the future. Many herbal medicines that were scientifically decried just a few years ago, because the science of the time could not understand how they worked, are now accepted as powerful medicines because scientific understanding has moved on. Acupuncture cannot be adequately explained by Western science, yet major surgery has been performed on conscious patients using only acupuncture for anaesthetic.

The concepts of Chi, Jing and Jin have been used to teach Tai Chi Chuan and the internal arts for hundreds of years and, whether the traditional explanation of what is happening is 'correct' in terms of our Western viewpoint or not, there can be no doubt that the training techniques offer great benefits, both medical and martial. Whether you believe in the existence of Chi or prefer to attribute effects in the internal arts to some other, as yet not fully explained, phenomena it is wisest, in my opinion, to proceed with an open mind and follow the traditional practices without worrying too much about what the 'reality' behind them is. Reality, in my experience, can also be subjective.

The bottom line is that it doesn't matter too much what the explanation for a training technique is, it's whether or not it works that counts.

Roundness

When you were first shown the movements of the Tai Chi Chuan Form you now practise you were almost certainly shown what is often called the 'square' version of the movement. This is because, as mentioned earlier, Tai Chi Chuan Forms are in fact one long movement from beginning to end and are very difficult to grasp in this manner. Therefore most teachers reduce the movements, first to a series of postures and then to a simplified version of each posture to make teaching, and learning, easier. Having learned the postures and the sequence the next job is to round out each movement to its correct form.

Master Lam used to say 'Everything in Tai Chi Chuan is a circle. Even when you think something is straight it's not.' To the eyes of the beginner this may be hard to understand. Sure, Tai Chi Chuan looks rounded but surely this kick or that punch are straight lines. During the next stage of your training you should begin to see the circularity in all aspects of Tai Chi Chuan.

Before you can effectively round out the movement of the Form between postures, the postures themselves and the structure of the body must be rounded. We looked at five of these, so called, 'posture considerations' in the first part of this book. Now we need to add another five. The complete set are:

1. Suspension of the head
2. Centring of the coccyx
3. Rounding of the shoulders
4. Rounding of the knees
5. Sinking of the elbows
6. Rounding of the Kua
7. Lifting of the back
8. Loosening of the chest
9. Sheltering of the stomach
10. Separating empty and solid.

Refer to p. 25 for advice on the first five, We'll take the next five, one at a time.

Incorrect front stance with the Kua un-rounded.

Correct front stance with rounded Kua.

6. **Rounding the Kua:** the Kua is the area at the top of the inner thighs formed in the execution of all postures using Tai Chi Chuan footwork. It's a common error to allow the knees to sag in and this leads to a square and unstable stance. The knees should be pushed out slightly on each movement so that this area is gently rounded. This means that if the right leg is forward in a front stance, it is the inside crescent of the right big toe that will be visible when you look down. The action of rounding the Kua tends to make the feet feel as if they are locked to the floor on every step and will make the posture feel stronger and more stable. At first, it may also feel more awkward when moving from one posture to another but this feeling will disappear once you are used to relaxing during the movement.

7. **Lifting the Back:** lifting the back is a more difficult manoeuvre to grasp. The point that needs to be lifted is the mid-shoulder blade point; this is an acupuncture point on the Du or governor meridian that runs up the back. It is located midway between the shoulder blades about four inches down from the base of the neck (this will vary from person to person due to differing builds). In order to lift this point it is necessary to focus on it while performing the postures and consciously lift the back. The effect of this will be to further straighten the spine and increase stability in each posture.

8. **Loosening of the Chest:** when the shoulders are relaxed and the back is lifted the chest naturally loosens. Relax your chest muscles while executing movements and be sure to breathe from the Tan Tien using the lower abdominal muscles and not the chest. Stiffness in the chest slows movement and retards the flow of energy.

9. **Sheltering the Stomach:** the stomach is located below the liver, starting on the left side of the body, extending through the middle and on to the right. At its lowest point it is about 2 inches above the belly button. This posture consideration is in fact taken care of by the combined actions of lifting the back and loosening the chest.

10. **Separating Empty and Solid:** this posture consideration is the most difficult to accomplish. It is the consideration of all movement as a collection of empty and solid or soft and hard parts, so that the entire movement is seen and felt as a shifting progression of empty and solid rather than as a set of postures and joining movements. This aspect is more appropriately covered in the advanced section.

It's important not to try to incorporate all these considerations at once. It's much better to work on one at a time until you can do the Form with all of them in place. Don't rush this process, be prepared to take as long as necessary to incorporate each of the considerations, even if this is several weeks or even months for each one. Think of this level as laying the foundations for Tai Chi Chuan, do the job well and the whole thing will be stronger and more enduring.

Tips to Help with Applying the Posture Considerations

Probably the best approach to developing the posture considerations is to start with the major postures themselves and practise them while concentrating on a particular consideration. Then begin practising the

Form while concentrating on that particular consideration. While practising the Form, halt your movement regularly to check that the new consideration, and all previously learned ones, are still in place, correcting your movement as you go along. This process will probably take longer than you think. Most people cannot accomplish it properly in less than a year of dedicated work. The last of the considerations, separating empty and solid, will be an ongoing work so don't be surprised if you find yourself coming back to it for as long as you practise Tai Chi Chuan and finding new depths in which to apply it.

Roundness as a Whole

There are two approaches to acquiring Roundness as a whole, both of them equally valid. One approach is to concentrate on the above posture considerations until you have them near enough right (80 per cent or more) and then focus on rounding the movement. The other is to split your training time so that you can work on both aspects together.

If you have time for six rounds of the Form you'll need to do one round to get yourself settled, then you could use two to practise a posture consideration as described above and the next two to work on Roundness in the movement, finishing your training with one more round done mindfully but without concern for any one particular element. You should make a mental note of deficiencies and mistakes but not stop to correct them.

Developing Roundness in the Movement

Whichever approach you decide to take in rounding the movement you should follow the advice of your instructor. Due to the differences in styles, specific advice cannot be given on how particular movements should be done, but here is some general advice.

Roundness of movement is developed by learning to physically generate each movement from the core of the body (the Tan Tien) rather than from the external parts of the body (the arms and legs). While trying to acquire Roundness in the movement of the Form it's a good idea to make the movement a little bigger than you would normally. Fill the space and make your movement full and rounded. Imagine you are like a 'Michelin Tyre Man', big and rounded and made of balloons. Don't allow your limbs to be too bent (but not dead straight either). A good tip is to imagine you have balloons between your legs, under your armpits and so on and to 'inflate' your movement.

There is a traditional saying in Tai Chi Chuan: 'Expanding, my circles fill the universe; rolling up I can hide them in my sleeve'.[6] This saying alludes to the fact that in Tai Chi Chuan we must all start out using big obvious circles, to develop the movement and the power within the movement. Once this has been done it is possible to internalize your circles until your movement is much more subtle and sophisticated. On no account should you try to develop small circles before you have developed big ones.

As you move, be aware that the movement of the postures of the Form follows the natural swing of the body. For instance, while turning to the right into a ward off (Peng) position, if you were to let your arm relax completely and do the movement fast, the centrifugal force would tend to make your arm end up close to where it would be while doing the technique. This is because all movements in Tai Chi Chuan are circular and follow the natural alignment of the body. All it requires to make the techniques out of the natural circular movement that the body generates is our own intention to make them happen. While working on this you should discover the circular nature of all movements in Tai Chi Chuan, even the ones that look like straight lines.

Inevitably while trying to identify the circles within Tai Chi Chuan you will get carried away and add circles where there shouldn't be any, making your movement flowery. Don't be overly concerned about this in the early stages, you can always eradicate the superfluous movements later on, but try to apply the best of your understanding to discern the natural circles within Tai Chi Chuan. As your understanding of the techniques contained in the movements improves, your ability to discern genuine circles from fanciful ones will improve also.

Roundness and Push Hands

An important tool for rounding the Form and improving posture is Push Hands. As you start to absorb the posture considerations into your form you will find your stance in Push Hands improves. Similarly, working to improve your Push Hands technique from your knowledge of the posture considerations will help you to improve your movement in the Form. As you practise Push Hands pay special attention to your posture and also to the roundness of your movement. Very quickly you'll discover that by improving the roundness in your techniques you can apply more power with less muscular effort, it will also help you to discover which circles in the movement are necessary and which are superfluous.

Supplementary Exercises

During the acquisition of Roundness it is a good idea to work on increasing your general flexibility and mobility. This will help you when you are using deeper stances and bigger movements and will generally improve your Form. The same advice on the practice of stretching exercises remains true so reread from the previous section if you need to. Your teacher will no doubt set you some new exercises but a useful selection has been added in Appendix IV at the back of this book.

Internal Circles

Within the Nei Kung there is a practice for internally circulating Chi that, whilst being circulated, is refined into Jing. This period of training, while working on external circularity, is the ideal time to begin work on this internal circulation, as it can take a long time to complete. If you are already training in the Nei Kung, this practice will probably crop up and you should learn it from your teacher. If not, you will probably find it difficult to grasp but it is something that can be practised even without training in the other aspects of the Nei Kung and it is particularly good for the health.

Known as the Small and Greater Heavenly Circles (called by some the Micro and Macro Cosmic Orbits), these techniques are designed to circulate energy by using your intent and awareness. Only the practice of the Small Heavenly Circle (SHC) is described here as the Greater Heavenly Circle really requires instruction from a teacher who can answer questions for you and guide your practice.

In classical Chinese theory, before birth, that is, in the womb, energy is derived from the umbilical cord (close to the Tan Tien) on an in breath and circulated round the perineum and up the spine to the top of the infant's head before circulating down the front of the body on the out breath (also out through the umbilical cord), in so doing generating pre-natal Chi that is stored in the body for use

Stretching exercise: the
Swing Kick Stretch.

throughout the individual's life. Once born, the cycle is reversed with energy being drawn in through the nose and circulating over the head and down the back on the in breath, then up the front of the body and out of the nose or mouth on the out breath, gradually depleting the body's store of pre-natal Chi. All this circulation takes place along the Ren and Du meridians, discussed earlier.

The practice of the Small and Greater Heavenly Circles is primarily to reverse the post-natal cycle so that the energy is once again circulated from the Tan Tien, round the perineum and up the back on the in breath and down the front of the body on the out breath. Though it's not deemed possible to make more pre-natal Chi, it is possible to make Jing, or refined Chi, which lengthens life expectancy and can be used in the martial arts.

Even if you're sceptical about the existence of Chi, it's worth practising the SHC as the mental discipline and focus required to accomplish the effects are of great worth in Tai Chi Chuan.

Reverse Breathing

In order to make the SHC more effective, there is a breathing technique that can be used alongside it known as reverse breathing. So far you have been breathing into the Tan Tien, using the lower abdominal muscles to expand this area in order to draw air into the lungs, thus allowing the upper abdomen and chest to remain relaxed. Reverse breathing involves contracting the lower abdominal muscles and expanding the mid-abdominal muscles, using the belly button as the midway point, on the in breath and contracting the mid-abdominal muscles while expanding the lower abdominal muscles on the out breath. The idea is to mimic the action of drawing in energy from the umbilicus. This practice almost certainly gives rise to apocryphal stories of Tai Chi Chuan practitioners actually breathing through their Tan Tien, which is of course impossible.

The action of this reverse breathing is very powerful and helps to stimulate the Chi in the Tan Tien, making it more volatile and easier to move.

Circulating Energy Round the Small Heavenly Circle

This practice can be done in just about any position but to begin with, either standing or sitting with a straight back is best. Remember to keep the tongue lightly pressed against the upper palate, just behind the teeth throughout, as the governor meridian, that runs up the back from the perineum and over the head to the mid-eyebrow point, goes deeper inside the body from there and terminates on the palate or roof of the mouth, meets the Functional meridian that begins in the tip of the tongue and runs down the front of the body, through the genital area, and terminates at the perineum.

Begin by relaxing as much as you can and focusing your concentration on your breathing in the Tan Tien. If you can maintain the reverse breathing technique discussed earlier, so much the better but don't worry if you can't. Breathe quietly through your nose; there's no need to take particularly deep breaths, just breathe naturally.

Having allowed yourself to relax and focused your attention on your Tan Tien for a few minutes you may begin to experience some feeling there that wasn't there when you started. Don't worry about what that experience might be, everyone is different and it would serve no useful purpose to describe common experiences to you. All you're looking for is a change of state from the time you started. It may take you a few attempts to feel anything at all but don't be disheartened, this is quite common. When you do experience something different in the Tan Tien, try to channel that feeling to the next point on the circle, the perineum, on each out breath. Again continue until you experience a different feeling at the perineum from how it was when you started focusing there. At first, you will most probably not be able to continue any further so, after consolidating the energy at the perineum point for a little while, return to the Tan Tien and focus there for a while again, in order to stabilize yourself before finishing.

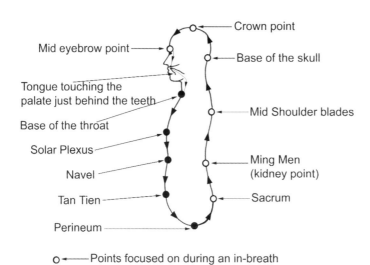

A diagram of the path taken by energy around the body during the Small Heavenly Circle.

When you can transfer the energy easily to the perineum from the Tan Tien it's time to move on to the next point on the SHC which is at the top of the Sacrum at the Sacral vertebrae. This time you move the energy on the in breath, again focusing your attention on the point until you feel a change of sensation of experience at the new point. When you've consolidated the energy there, return it to the Tan Tien before finishing.

The process continues with each major point around the circle. These are, from the perineum up: the sacral vertebrae, the Ming Men in the centre of the back, the point between the shoulder blades, the Jade Pillow at the base of the skull, the crown point at the top of the head, and the mid-eyebrow point. With all these points the energy is transferred on the in breath; focus on the movement of energy to the next point on the in breath only, do nothing on the out breath.

When you can reach the mid-eyebrow point the second half of the circle kicks in. Transfer the energy to the point at the base of the throat where the clavicles meet, via the palate and tongue, but do this on the out breath. Again you're looking for a change of feeling from the time you began to focus. You may experience some difficulty in getting past the palate, due to its bony nature, so you'll need to be persistent.

From the base of the throat the next point is at the solar plexus, then on to the navel and from there you can take the energy all the way back to the Tan Tien. All these points are done on the out breath, on the in breath just relax.

When you can transfer the energy all the way around the SHC and have practised it point by point for a few weeks, the next step is to try to circulate the energy around the SHC in one breath. That is to say on

an out breath you can shift the energy to the perineum from the Tan Tien, on the next in breath you can shift the energy all the way up the back, over the head, and to the mid eyebrow point and on the next out breath you can shift the energy back down to the perineum. Eventually you should be able to circulate the energy around the SHC breath after breath. When you can do that, continue to practise it as a regular part of your training. Before you get to that stage of course you'll need to practise the individual points one at a time, probably for a long time even after you've managed to get a complete circulation. Traditionally, this practice is said to take 100 days to accomplish but it often takes much, much longer.

Things to be Aware of When Practising the Small Heavenly Circle

The Chinese have an expression that translates as 'watch the cooking time'. What this relates to is that things must be done at the right time in order to get the best results. Cook something for too long and it will be ruined, don't cook it for long enough and it will be raw. When trying to move between points on the SHC you need to allow the sensation to build up to just the right amount before moving to the next point. Too long and the feeling will dissipate, not long enough and the energy will peter out before reaching the next point. You can only discover the correct amount of time through practice and experience. Don't worry when you get it wrong, it's all part of the learning curve.

The feelings you have at each point while working on the SHC may vary. Don't be too concerned about what the feeling is, just be aware of the change in the experience. Some people feel the energy move between points but most only feel the difference in feeling at each point, it really doesn't matter which applies to you as there's no advantage or disadvantage either way.

While focusing on different points around the SHC you may involuntarily tense muscles around the point you're trying to focus on. When you catch yourself doing this make a conscious effort to relax. Tension in the muscles will retard the flow of energy and the act of tensing muscles around a point may cause you to mistake the tension for a change in feeling.

Warning: until you can circulate energy all the way around the SHC and back to the Tan Tien retrace your steps at the end of your practice session and focus on the Tan Tien before finishing. This is very important as energy that is left in the wrong place can stagnate, causing illness or leaving the body prone to injury.

Sexual Practice with the Nei Kung

It's not my intention to deal with this subject in detail, it would require a book all to itself and, in my opinion, should really only be taught by a personal teacher. However, if you haven't had instruction in the conservation of energy in sexual practice the next best advice is to be temperate in your sex life, particularly while trying to accomplish the SHC. Some sources would advise celibacy, especially while trying to complete the SHC, though this may be taking things too far for many people and may not be possible or desirable for people in a committed relationship. Overindulgence in sexual practice, without the ability to conserve energy, will make the SHC very difficult to complete, however, and should be avoided. It can also lead to lower back pain and pain in the kidney region.

Continuity

When you have rounded the postures and movement of your Form to a point where it is deemed by your teacher to be sufficient for your current purposes (normally about 80 per cent correct), it's time to move on to the next major training principle, that of Continuity. A word of warning though. It's important to retain the Roundness you've acquired in your Form; keep paying attention to Roundness while you train the next stage so you don't lapse back into the square version of the Form.

Constant Rate

Adding Roundness to your movement imparted other skills and abilities and the same is true of continuity. The purpose of this training is to help you to co-ordinate your movements and postures. It's a central tenet of Tai Chi Chuan that 'when one part (of the body) moves, all parts (of the body) move'. To achieve this end, training at this point shifts to moving at a constant rate.

Constant rate means that you practise the Form from beginning to end with a new evenness of movement, ensuring that each posture and each joining movement are as smooth as possible and that their speed of execution is constant throughout the Form. To achieve this you may have to speed up your movement just a little, in order to allow you to keep a constant speed without pausing or becoming stiff.

Practitioners of Chen style Tai Chi Chuan may be thinking: 'Ah!, but Chen style has both fast and slow movements within the Form.' This is true but it is still possible to practise with Continuity. What is required is that all slow movements are of a consistent speed relative to one another and also all fast movements are of a consistent speed relative to one another.

Coordination

The whole body, mind and spirit should ultimately coordinate together throughout the entire movement of Tai Chi Chuan. However, at this stage our main concern is with the coordination of the body.

To make coordination easier to incorporate into your movement it is often split up into ten essential points, though only the first six of these are important at this stage, they are:

1. **The head must coordinate with the coccyx:** the crown of the head should, at all times, be in line with the bones of the coccyx (that are lightly tucked in, in accordance with the earlier posture training). This is so there is a solid and continuous link from the hips up which enables the transmission of energy along the spine without stiffness.

Brush Knee, body correctly aligned in forward-leaning posture.

   The principle of keeping the back straight in this manner has given rise to some argument amongst Tai Chi Chuan practitioners as to whether or not it means that the back should be vertical throughout the movement. In fact this is not an issue. As long as the back is straight from the crown of the head to the coccyx throughout, it really doesn't matter whether the body is vertical or inclined in a particular movement – for example, some schools of Tai Chi Chuan incline the body forward in the movement 'Brush Knee and Twist Step' while others keep the body vertical. Both are correct provided the body does not bend. In the end it comes down more to the application of technique than to anything else.

2. **The neck must coordinate with the waist:** Chinese armies traditionally had a system of flags and banners with

Brush Knee, body correctly aligned in vertical posture.

Brush Knee, incorrect posture, bad alignment.

which orders were transmitted to troops. In the Classics of Tai Chi Chuan the waist is likened to a banner, in that, the turning force of the body is transmitted up the trunk by the action of the waist. If the neck is kept in coordination with the waist the transmission of turning force will be smooth and without effort.

3. **The shoulders must coordinate with the Kua:** as the Kua opens and closes in each movement, so the shoulders must mirror that movement. For example, in the movement 'Ward Off Right', as the body turns to the right and the right hand comes up, the rotation and opening of the shoulder should take place in time with the opening of the Kua, neither leading nor lagging the movement.

4. **The elbows must coordinate with the knees:** the techniques of Tai Chi

Chuan use natural power, that is, power without stiffness or tension. The knees and elbows rotate together, in a harmonious manner, throughout the movement, mirroring the turning of one with the other.

5. **The shin of one leg must coordinate with the shin of the other:** in order to give the body stability and to effectively transmit force from the feet up to the rest of the body the legs must act as a unit. As the weight of the body shifts from one leg to the other the shins should act as a coordinated unit which makes a stable base for the transmission of power from the floor.

6. **The toes of one foot must coordinate with the toes of the other foot:** to achieve stability in motion the body's weight must be correctly distributed with each step. In order to accomplish this the direction of the feet must be in alignment with the movement of the torso.

The above six considerations are sufficient at this level of training, though for the purpose of completeness the other four will be included; you'll need to refer back to these later in your training.

7. **The Shen (Spirit) must coordinate with the mind:** the inner spirit of vitality, the essence of consciousness, must be aligned with the intent of the mind.

8. **Mind must coordinate with Jin:** the intent of the mind must be aligned with the refined intrinsic energy of the body.

9. **Jin must coordinate with Li (strength):** the refined, intrinsic energy of the body must be applied harmoniously with and aligned to the body's physical movement.

10. **The inner (Shen, Mind, Jin) must coordinate with the outer (first six principles).**

It's important not to mistake coordination with rigidity or uniformity when applying the first six considerations. Two people may coordinate their activities without necessarily doing exactly the same thing. Thus different parts of the body have their own functions to fulfil. The object is to coordinate their activities so that they complement and enhance the function of each other. For instance, in the movement 'Step Up, Parry, Punch', it is vital that the punch is delivered as the body's weight moves onto the leading leg (otherwise the punch will be without power). If the above coordination considerations are adhered to

Punch moving forward with body weight.

Step forward and parry.

the shins will coordinate, ensuring a stable basis for the transmission of power from the floor, the shoulders will be coordinating with the Kua, ensuring that the body turns and aligns at the right time and the elbows will be coordinating with the knees, ensuring that the punch is delivered as the body's weight moves onto the front leg. The other considerations are all just as important in this movement of course but the three mentioned best illustrate the example.

Training Coordination With Continuity

As with the training of Roundness, it's best to focus on one of the coordination

Punch delivered in coordination with whole body.

As Roundness begins to reveal the source of power inherent in the movements of Tai Chi Chuan, so Continuity and evenness begin to reveal the dynamic nature of the Form.

Slowness (Not Hurrying)

Ask what characterizes Tai Chi Chuan and most people will mention the slowness of the movements. Slowness, however, is a means to an end, not an end in itself. At this level of training practising slowly has two main purposes; to allow you time to focus on everything that's supposed to be incorporated in your Form and to develop a serene state of consciousness that will facilitate both the perfecting of the things you've already learned and the acquisition of new skills. Later in your training, if you are intent on learning Tai Chi Chuan as a martial art, you will find that a degree of serenity is essential when facing an opponent and can be one of the hardest things to apply in that situation.

The development of serenity is actually far more important than merely moving slowly. Tai Chi Chuan is a martial art and to be used as such means that the practitioner must, on occasion, move very quickly. It's just as important to remain serene when moving quickly as it is when moving slowly. In order to develop this state of consciousness, however, the method is to slow your movement down.

If you practise a modern 'Short Form', chances are that it takes about four to six minutes to perform at normal speed. During this phase of your training you should slow your Form down until you can comfortably execute it in between eight to ten minutes, while still retaining the elements you've so far incorporated. This may not sound too difficult but, apart from the difficulty of maintaining

considerations at a time in order to add them to your Form. To begin with it can be helpful to practise short sections of two or three movements, trying to make sure that the new consideration is incorporated throughout while maintaining everything previously covered. Again, be prepared to work longer on this than you might expect and don't be surprised if adding a new coordination consideration forces you to re-evaluate what you've already learned.

Continue until you can complete the Form with all the physical coordination considerations in place, at an even pace throughout and with the roundness and posture considerations correctly applied.

continuity at slower speeds, you're likely to find a certain mental resistance to practising slowly, and that resistance usually gets worse before it gets better. This is because it's in the nature of the mind to want to rush through things, particularly things it believes it already understands.

Typically, the first time you slow your Form down to around the 8-minute mark it won't feel too bad. Sure, you'll be aware of things that you need to work on but the experience won't be too painful and you may even feel a deep joy from practising slowly. As you continue to practise slowly day after day, however, it's quite likely that you'll find a growing irritation with the work and your mind will make you feel uncomfortable at having to work through the movements slowly. This is perfectly normal and part of the process of developing a serene state of consciousness. Developing this state of mind is essential before practising the movements slowly can be of real benefit to your Form.

Techniques for Developing Serenity and Slowness

If you are practising a form of Nei Kung, particularly if that Nei Kung practice includes static as well as moving postures, it will help you enormously while trying to get into the right state of mind. In fact in practising the Nei Kung you'll probably already have developed the state of mind you're looking for, so you'll just need to apply it to the Form. There's no point in trying to describe the state of mind you're after, such descriptions are rarely useful, suffice it to say that it is one in which you feel at ease, your thoughts are observed but not followed and your actions are led primarily by your awareness, rather than any analytical ability.

Whether you're practising the Nei kung or not there are a number of practices that can help you accomplish the state of mind you seek while practising the Form.

Affirmation

A simple and effective method of gaining control of your consciousness is simply to remind yourself before practising each day that you are in no hurry, that the whole point of this practice is to do the Form slowly and that you want to enjoy, even luxuriate in, the experience of doing the Form slowly. This simple technique is surprisingly effective in calming the mind, especially in the early stages of this practice.

Focusing on your Breathing

This is the ideal point to develop the breathing in your Form to align with the movement and many teachers will take the opportunity to add this skill to your repertoire at this point. Until now you've most likely been breathing into the Tan Tien but not trying to align the breathing with your movements. Now that you can perform the sequence of movements comfortably and have all this extra time in which to focus on them it should be safe to begin the alignment of breath and movement.

It's not possible in the medium of print to give a blow-by-blow account of the breathing in your Form. Apart from anything else, each Form will differ slightly. This is a job for your teacher but there are some general rules that, though not absolutes, will help to guide you in this task.

- **Continue to breathe into the Tan Tien:** it's important that you continue to use the lower abdominal muscles to control your breathing, otherwise you will develop stiffness in the chest or upper abdominal areas.

- **Breathe in on movements that receive energy:** such as 'Roll back' or 'Grasp Bird's Tail'.
- **Breathe out on movements that exert energy:** such as a push, thrust, punch or long kick, for example 'Separate Right and Left' or 'Step Up, Parry, Punch'.
- **Breathe in on backward steps and when the Kua is closing.**
- **Breathe out on forward steps and when the Kua is opening.**

There are some exceptions to these rules however, amongst them snapping kicks, such as 'Deflect Downward and Kick', which must be done on the in breath, so it's important to work closely with your teacher when aligning breathing to the movement.

Once the sequence and breathing align-ment has been learned and can be done without hesitation, continuing to concen-trate deeply on your breathing while allow-ing your awareness to control your movement will further help you to attain the right state of mind and slowing down your breathing will help to slow your movement.

Overloading Your Senses
It's very difficult to quieten the mind. Ever tried to stop thinking altogether, even for a minute? What's the first thing that happens if someone says 'Don't think of a monkey'? Yet, most esoteric practices revolve in some way around controlling the thought process.

One practice particularly effective for calming the mind is to give it more infor-mation than it can handle. Done properly it will calm down and take a back seat to your more intuitive consciousness and awareness.

Start by not allowing your eyes to focus on any one detail of your surroundings.

Try to fill your vision from one periphery to the other but don't concentrate on any single thing. Then do the same thing with your hearing. Try to listen to everything without focusing on any single sound. Include tactile sensations and at the same time concentrate on your breathing deep in the Tan Tien. Said quickly this may not sound too difficult but be prepared for a long period of practice before it becomes second nature.

There's no need to restrict the above technique to your practice of the Form. In fact it's best to learn the technique at another time and then apply it to your Form practice. An ideal way to acquire this ability is to practise it while walking, which is something you can do at almost any time.

A word of caution: it's best not to prac-tise this technique while driving, especially when you first start, as it can cause a degree of disorientation until you're used to it.

Eventually you'll be able to complete the Form without a care in the world and with a feeling of deep calm, however slowly or quickly you're called upon to complete the movement.

Body Lightness

One of the things that characterizes the movement of the novice in Tai Chi Chuan is the noise made while practising the Form. The scraping sound of Tai Chi shoes or the squeaking of trainers on the floor is the noise being referred to here. Done correctly, the Form should be almost silent, the only sound being made by the occasional movement that requires the foot to pivot while the body's weight is on it.

Most styles of Chinese martial arts have some kind of body lightness training. This training can range from elaborate physical exercises, such as jumping out of a waist-high pit using only the calf and ankle muscles, to esoteric internal practices. Body lightness training in Tai Chi Chuan is typically subtle and relies on both internal practice and step training.

If you've ever sat near the front during a performance of ballet, or better still if you've ever sat in on rehearsals of a ballet production when there's only a piano for accompaniment, you've most likely been surprised at the noise the performers make while dancing. Ballet, particularly when observed through the medium of television, looks effortlessly graceful but, while it is undoubtedly very graceful, it is far from effortless. In order to give the impression of lightness in movement the dancers exert tremendous force through their feet and hold their bodies very tightly to lift them up. A similar approach is taken by many external martial arts styles, particularly those that use high kicks and flamboyant jumping techniques such as Northern Shaolin. This is almost the exact opposite of the practice required in Tai Chi Chuan.

There is a saying: 'below the waist is the mountain, above the waist is the sky'. In Tai Chi Chuan it is the legs that form the solid base on which the light and effortless movements of the upper body take place. In order to develop lightness in the Form it is important to learn to sink the weight deeply into the legs and feet and then to cultivate a method of stepping that allows you to move your weight freely from posture to posture.

Internal Practice

If you practise the Nei Kung your teacher may well give you a practice for developing inner lightness. The following technique is very useful in this regard but will probably not be of much use to you if you have not already been trained in the Nei Kung.

This exercise is similar to the static Zhan Zhuang posture known as 'standing in the stream' where the arms are outstretched from the sides of the body, palms down, though they are raised a little higher. Feet are set one-and-a-half to two shoulder widths apart and the knees should be slightly bent. Begin by allowing your body to relax from the top down, consciously relax your face, chest, back, midsection, groin and thighs until it feels as if all your weight has sunk below your knees. Next raise your arms, palms down with the fingers spread out, on either side of your body until they are level with your solar plexus, as if your hands were resting on two large balls against which you can push gently, lifting your body. Focus the energy coming up through your hands to the point between the shoulder blades in the mid-back where it helps in the lifting of the upper body while the feet remain rooted to the floor with all the weight of the body concentrated in the calves and feet. Hold the position for five to ten minutes and practise at least once a day.

Points to remember when doing this exercise are: keep your tongue resting on the upper palate just behind the teeth, concentrate your breathing on the Tan Tien and consciously relax your upper body (particularly your shoulders and arms). If you've done Small Heavenly Circle (SHC) training and are quite well accomplished in this practice you can also try focusing your energy on the mid-shoulder blade point during the in breath cycle.

External Training

To help train you to sink your weight while lightening the upper body I recommend the use of ankle weights, although the way these weights are deployed is a little

Nei Kung position for aiding body lightness.

unusual. During the beginning of this training I get my students to wear their ankle weights, of between two and four pounds, all day long while they are not practising Tai Chi Chuan. Over a period of time this practice encourages a feeling of weight in the lower legs and, when the weights are removed during the practice of the Form, helps to encourage light stepping as the legs feel lighter by comparison.

Later the process is reversed and the weights are worn only during the practice of the Form. By this time you should have acquired the correct feeling of lightness in the upper body and be rooted in your feet, and the addition of ankle weights while training the Form will focus your mind on your stepping with the extra degree of difficulty making for rapid progress.

Step Training

During the practice of the internal and external training it's important to begin work on the way you step throughout the practice of your Form. The stepping technique is not complicated but it is difficult to do well. What it involves is relaxing your ankles and sinking into each step while focusing on transferring your weight correctly and completely before pivoting or moving from one posture to another so that the feet are not dragged or scraped on the floor. There are exceptions, such as in a movement where you must pivot on the heel of the front foot that is bearing most of the weight of the body – in many Forms this happens during 'Brush Knee and Twist Step', but even then the inner practice of lifting the upper body at the mid-shoulder blade point helps to make the movement lighter than it would otherwise be. Again this practice may take longer than you think to get right and you should be prepared to work on your stepping daily for some time until you can complete the Form with a light feeling, rooted at each step, with little or no sound being made by the feet on the floor, regardless of the footwear you use or the nature of the surface.

An auxiliary practise that helps in attaining the correct step is 'The Hero's Stroll'. This is basically a free-form stepping exercise, using all the steps of the Form but without the hand movements to distract you. Often this practice is given to beginners, sometimes at the first class, but it is most useful at this point, when you wish to improve your step and other elements of the Form are already in place.

Place your hands on your hips or leave them loose at your sides. Stand with your feet shoulder width apart. Bend your knees to lower your stance to the level that you would use when practising the Form and step forward onto the heel of your left foot, extending the leg so that it is almost but not quite straight. Move your weight forward into a front stance, trying to observe all the posture considerations that you have previously learned. Pay special

Hero's Stroll 1.

Hero's Stroll 2.

Hero's Stroll 3.   Hero's Stroll 4.   Hero's Stroll 5.

attention to relaxing the ankles and rooting your weight in the feet while at the same time lifting the upper body internally at the mid-shoulder blade point. When your weight has settled, move forward, shifting more of your weight onto your left leg until you can lift your right foot and bring it in to your left ankle, then continue to move your right foot forward and out in an arc till it is extended but not quite straight, heel touching the floor, before shifting your weight onto the right foot, and so on. All the steps in the Form can be practised in this way, including twisting steps, turns, sweeping steps and pull downs, for example, 'Single Whip Down'. At all times, with the exception of pull downs, your eye line should remain level and the scenery should not 'bob up and down' as you move, as if you are being pulled along by an invisible cord from the Tan Tien, where the movement emanates from.

Relaxed Force

The term Sung Jin translates as relaxed force. The literal translation of Sung, however, is of hair that is left to hang loose, not braided or bound. So the idea of Sung is one of fullness and looseness, without restraint or tension.

By this point in your training you should be beginning to develop Sung Jin, though it may be a while before it develops sufficiently to be useful in a martial sense. Without developing Sung Jin it is impossible to use any other form of Jin or internal force. This is because muscular tension inhibits the flow of force through the body and then only localized power is possible, instead of whole body power. Indeed when Sung Jin is sufficiently developed the techniques of Tai Chi Chuan start to become effective, even without developing any other level of internal power.

There is no great secret to Sung Jin. It is the natural and total power of the body when it is unrestrained by tension, resistance, uncoordinated or clumsy movement. If you have worked through to this point, and that means trained all the principles until they are second nature to you and not just intellectually absorbed them, Sung Jin will be beginning to manifest in your movement.

It's good to be aware that this is an important ability to cultivate. Often Sung Jin is misunderstood because it is simple and subtle. The mind always wants to apply more physical effort where less can actually be more effective.

Perfecting the principles already covered will help develop Sung Jin, as will partner work such as Push Hands and other forms of sparring, but it will develop quickest if you are consciously trying to develop it in all your movement. Remember: the less, the more.

Related Practice for the Elementary Section

Over the years it takes to cover the material in the elementary section you will no doubt be introduced to several other training practices, either directly or indirectly associated with your practice of Tai Chi Chuan. Different styles and individual teachers will have their own practices that enhance the learning of Tai Chi Chuan and I have no wish to second-guess what those may be. The elements mentioned in this section are either typical of those used by teachers of Tai Chi Chuan or are things that I am particularly fond of and have found to work well.

Before moving on to related practices, this is probably an ideal time to point out that anyone who is learning Tai Chi Chuan just for the health benefits it offers and who has no interest in the martial arts has probably covered all that is necessary for this purpose. Of course, if you continue to practise Tai Chi Chuan, and you won't continue to get the health benefits if you don't, you'll probably absorb more simply by being involved in the art but, fundamentally, all you need in order to gain these benefits you already know if you've trained to this point.

Double Push Hands

Whether you're interested in the martial aspects of Tai Chi Chuan or not, Push Hands practice is a prerequisite for developing skill and enhancing progress. There are elements of Tai Chi Chuan that may well be impossible to learn without practising Push Hands and practising it properly at that. Push hands is an exercise in sensitivity and the application of the Tai Chi principle, not just a technique for developing fighting skill, and without it many aspects of the art will simply not develop.

It's helpful to have at least a basic understanding of the martial techniques of Tai Chi Chuan when practising Push Hands, again whether you're interested in the

Double Push Hands white shirt begins to deflect push.

White shirt pushes back, black shirt begins deflection.

Black shirt completes deflection and begins to push back.

Black shirt pushes, white shirt begins deflection to the left.

White shirt completes left deflection.

White shirt pushes back.

martial arts or not, because without some understanding of how the movements are supposed to be applied it's very difficult to make much use of Push Hands training. Moreover it could get very boring!

At some point during your practice of Roundness or Continuity you'll most likely graduate from single to double Push Hands. The purpose and principles are the same but now both hands come into play during all the technique and the movement becomes more sophisticated. Refer back to the section on Push Hands in the first chapter for the basic principles of Push Hands training, they still apply here.

We won't go into the practice of double Push Hands in detail, indeed there are several forms of it that could be described, but the sequence of photographs on pages 70–71 showing a common type of fixed step double Push Hands with some

emphasis on the application of technique and short descriptions with the sequence.

During the time it takes to cover this part of your training you'll spend many hours practising Push Hands with one or many partners. The best progress is always made with partners who are at a similar level of training to yourself. It's always good to practise with someone just a little more experienced than yourself as it will stretch your ability but there's no point in training with someone who's had many more years of practice than you as you'll generally be unable to keep up with them or to understand why you can't make your techniques work and you'll learn little and may become discouraged. That's not to say it's not good to have the occasional bout with someone who's much more experienced, such as your teacher perhaps. As you wouldn't expect to do too well against such a person, you shouldn't get

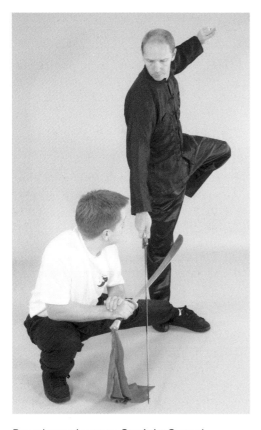

Broadsword verses Straight Sword.

though many great masters also studied and taught the spear, and the pole technique in Tai Chi Chuan is close to spear technique in any case. These days, however, many teachers incorporate other weapons into the training of Tai Chi Chuan and, provided the weapon can be adapted to the principles of Tai Chi Chuan, there's no real problem with this, except from the point of view of the traditionalist.

Weapons training can help you to improve your balance, footwork, spatial awareness, hand–eye coordination and stamina. These days you can even spar safely with weapons, thanks to foam-covered swords and other safety equipment, and that can give you a real insight into making the weapon an extension of your body.

Although weapons have extra considerations beyond the hand Form they are, essentially, practised in the same way, and all the same principles apply. Weapons training, though mainly aesthetic (at least as far as swords are concerned) in this day and age, adds another dimension to training in Tai Chi Chuan.

disheartened but may, in fact, be inspired. Likewise it's not good to train for long periods with partners who have much less experience than you. While it may be good for your ego it won't help your technique.

As well as fixed step Push Hands, where you don't move your feet other than to perhaps raise the toes of the front foot or do the occasional sliding step up or back, there's also single step Push Hands and free step Push Hands as you progress.

Weapons Training
Traditionally Tai Chi Chuan practitioners study only three types of weapon: the pole, the straight sword and the broadsword,

Self-Defence – Part Two
Some teachers will offer another, simpler, form of martial art for the martially inclined student, to provide effective techniques until the time when Tai Chi Chuan can be utilized in a combat situation. But even when this option is available a self-defence curriculum is still useful, both for martially inclined students and for those who simply want to be able to defend themselves in times of dire need. This topic was introduced in the related practices section of Chapter 1 (pages 42–45) and it is essential that these pages be reread before continuing. It may also be of use to reread the section on breakfalls, as

Black shirt attempts a standing front strangle or head butt.

White shirt steps back drawing the attacker in.

falling tends to be an inevitable consequence of this type of training.

There follow some self-defence techniques that I have found to be particularly effective over the years. They are based on techniques and principles from a number of disciplines including: Tai Chi Chuan, Choy Lee Fut, Chin Na, Shiao Chiao and Ju Jitsu.

Standing front strangle release: While it is true that this attack is almost never used by a man against another man and only rarely by a man against a woman, it is an attack that many systems do not deal with well and the technique shown here will just as easily work on someone who is grabbing your collar and attempting to head-butt you. As the attacker lunges forward to grab your neck or collar, step back with your left leg, allowing the attacker to take hold but moving with him. At the same time, swing your right arm up high and arc it down to your left side, bringing your left hand up to catch the attacker's hands against your body. The release from the strangle is effected by your armpit (an unusual weapon but effective in this instance) rolling the force of your attacker's arms away. This will have the effect of uprooting your attacker and before he can regain his balance, swing your right fist (palm down so that the clenched muscles between the little finger and wrist are moving toward the attacker) in an arc through your attacker's neck (don't aim for the surface of the neck but bring the arm right through the target) making contact with your forearm, fist or, if the attacker is still much closer, with the back of your elbow. NB This is a devastating blow and will result in serious injury or death if used without restraint. Do not try this on family or friends. The swing punch can be practised on a hanging bag.

White shirt completes right arm swing, unbalancing the attacker.

White shirt swings back, striking the attacker behind the ear.

White shirt follows through as the attacker is knocked down.

Wrist grab release: Even someone very strong who grabs your wrist can be dislodged using this technique, which nicely sets up the attacker for counterstrikes. In

the example shown, the attacker grasps the defender's right wrist with his left hand and prepares to punch with his right hand. As soon as the grip is on, the defender steps diagonally forward with his right foot, at the same time swinging his right arm in an arc with the palm starting off facing downward and finishing facing upward, using his body rather than his arm to power the movement. Simultaneously the defender's left hand inscribes the opposite arc, ending up just in front of his right hand against the attacker's forearm. NB It is important to keep the right arm moving forward and not try to pull it back. At the zenith of the movement the defender's wrist easily escapes the grip, no matter how strong, through the weak point between the attacker's thumb and forefinger. Even if the attacker starts to throw the punch it will be diverted by a combination of the swinging movement and the intercepting hands. Once the grip is released

Black shirt seizes white shirt's arm and is ready to punch.

White shirt steps diagonally in, and swings arm up to effect release and neutralization of punch.

White shirt steps diagonally left, controlling the attacker's arm.

White shirt strikes attacker behind the ear with a palm heel.

Detail showing the weak point between attacker's thumb and forefinger.

Detail showing thumb and elbow lock.

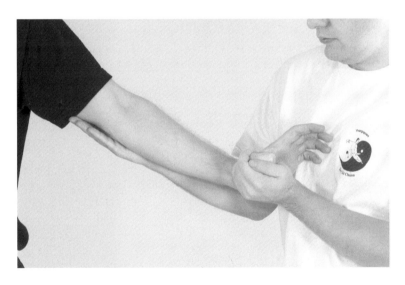

the defender immediately steps diagonally to the left, toward the attacker, controlling the attacker's left hand with his left hand and strikes with the heel of his or her palm at the attacker's neck, just below their left ear, following up with kicks, strikes and a takedown as necessary.

Clothing grip release: In this example the attacker grasps the defender's shirt with his left hand to pull him on to a punch. The defender steps away with his left foot into a horse stance and brings his right arm up and round to strike into the attacker's left elbow. Simultaneously the defender slams his left palm into the attacker's thumb at the grip (which is extraordinarily painful and will release the grip on the shirt) following which he grips the attacker's, probably broken, thumb in

Black shirt grab's white shirt's clothes and prepares to punch.

White shirt steps away, locking the attacker's thumb and arm.

Black shirt is unbalanced and drawn in, white shirt strikes the attacker's groin, keeping the lock on his thumb.

his palm. The attacker's punch is neutralized by the combination of the defender's change of position and the action of his elbow being struck forward, upsetting his balance. Having gained control of the situation, the defender slides in deep behind the attacker and at the same time swings his fist down into the attacker's groin before dropping him by the simple means of applying a downward pressure to the attacker's left hip that is checked by the defender's thigh. Follow up with such strikes as may be necessary.

Half-Nelson release: In this example, the attacker grasps the defender around the neck with his right arm using his left arm as a lever to increase the pressure on the defender's windpipe. The defender immediately slaps the attacker's elbow with his right palm and twists his neck to the right to make use of the small gap on

White shirt takes the attacker down.

BELOW LEFT: Black shirt applies a Half Nelson.

BELOW: White shirt creates a breathing space in the crook of the attacker's arm.

the inside of the elbow and afford some breathing space. The defender slides his right foot to his right and shifts his weight to the right, simultaneously striking back with his left fist into the attacker's groin (uprooting the attacker by bringing him up

White shirt steps to the right and strikes the groin.

White shirt twists and drops to his right, pulling down.

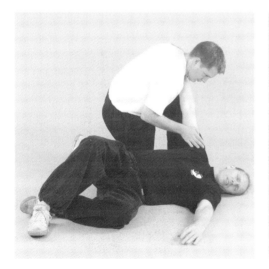

The attacker is flipped over and white shirt strikes his face.

White shirt twists to his left pinning the attacker and striking.

on his toes). The defender then smoothly twists to his left, dropping down on his right knee as tight in to the attacker as possible, at the same time pulling down on the attacker's right arm so as to cause the attacker to flip over the top of his body.

NB The defender doesn't throw the attacker by using his body in the Judo sense, he merely creates a space for the attacker to fall into and overbalances him in that direction.

Once the attacker is down, the defender swivels to his left and squats down with his left knee across the attacker's neck and the attacker's right arm (locked at the elbow joint) across his right thigh. (Note that kneeling too heavily on the neck can be fatal.) The left hand remains free to deliver such strikes as may be necessary with hammer fist or palm to the attacker's face, neck and groin.

Appropriate striking areas and body weapons for self-defence: As already mentioned, applying self-defence tech-niques isn't like applying a martial art. The hands are not usually conditioned and there is no great skill (as yet) to rely on when facing an attacker. Due to this, it's best to rely on strikes that don't require any particular conditioning of the hands or feet and only to attack areas of the body that are likely to be vulnerable. The main areas to avoid trying to attack are the chest and abdomen and the back. While it's true that certain techniques can do great dam-age in these areas, they all require a focus and power that will not usually be available to the novice. Trying to elbow someone in the solar plexus, perhaps through well-conditioned abdominal muscles or a thick coat or jacket will yield little effect without great accuracy and power. It is far better to stick to vulnerable areas, some of which are not thought of as targets (like twisting the fingers) and that can be severely dam-aged with little effort and the element of surprise. There follow some examples of typical body weapons of self-defence, to-gether with examples of appropriate target areas.

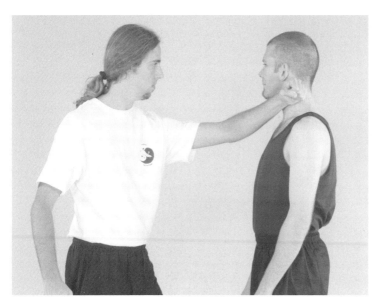

Outside hammer-fist strike.

Inside hammer-fist strike.

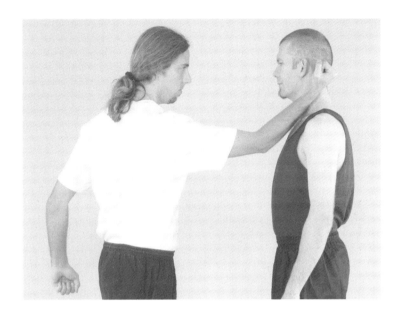

Inside and outside hammer-fist strikes: The hammer-fist utilizes the bottom of a clenched fist and can also include the lower forearm as part of the weapon. These strikes are particularly effective against the neck (where arteries that feed the brain and the windpipe are housed, not to mention the weakest part of the spine), the groin and behind the ears. **Note:** Any strike to the neck can potentially be fatal.

Descending hammer-fist strike: This is the same as inside and outside hammer-fist but swung from above. This technique

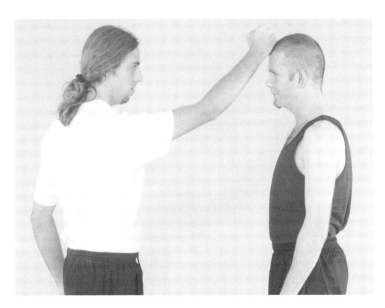

Downward hammer-fist strike.

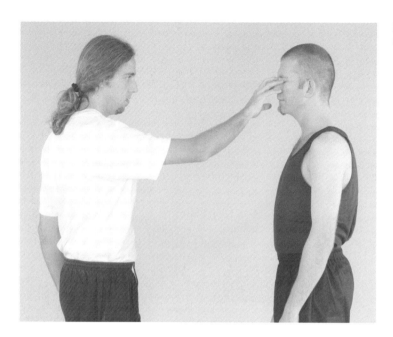

Bent finger strike
or gouge.

is particularly useful against the top of the head and the nose.

Stiff, bent finger strikes: By keeping the splayed fingers as stiff as possible but slightly bent they become a formidable weapon against the eyes and throat. **Note:** Jabs to the eyes/throat can be dangerous, even fatal. It is very important to keep the fingers slightly bent so that they can

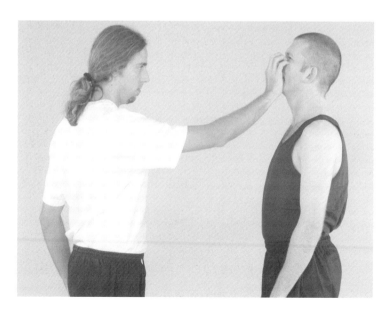

Palm heel strike.

collapse a little on contact (particularly on contact with anything hard or strong), which will save you breaking them if you encounter more resistance than you expect.

Palm heel strike: The palm heel is a much better weapon than the fist for most people. Although it sacrifices a couple of inches of reach, it is far stronger than most people's fists and can pack a mighty blow. Best of all, while it may become bruised, it will not break, as knuckles are prone to do when encountering solid bone. It is an ideal follow-up to a bent finger strike, catching the jaw or nose, and can be used against almost any target.

Front and back elbow strikes: The elbow is a formidable weapon. Although only of use at very close range it has a strong mechanical advantage and can deliver tremendous power. Ideally used against the neck, head and groin, it is possible to augment the power of an elbow strike by pushing the fist with the other palm. NB Never use the tip of the elbow as this can be easily damaged against hard surfaces.

Clapping the ears: Clapping the ears with the palms can be very effective as this technique can cause burst ear drums. Such a clap can be delivered with a single hand as well as with both hands, as illustrated. For maximum effect the palms should be kept cupped as this increases the air pressure in the aural cavity. **Potentially dangerous.**

Chopping and knife hand: The edge of the hand can be used with great effect against the throat, either in the commonly seen 'chopping' motion (though this is often easy to see coming and to block) and

Front forearm strike.

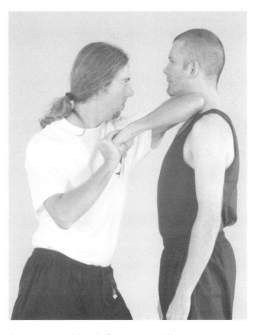

Augmented back forearm strike.

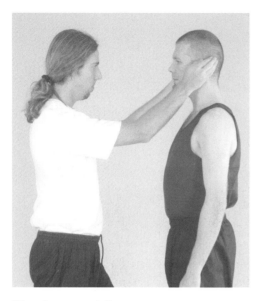

Clapping ears strike.

also as a straight thrust, turning the hand out so that the edge of the hand catches the throat at an angle. **Potentially dangerous.**

Low side kick: Under the right circumstances and with a little practice this kick can be very effective, both in unbalancing an attacker and also in breaking or dislocating the knee joint (both very debilitating injuries). It also has the advantage of keeping the attacker at a distance.

Front heel kick: Another long-range technique, the snapping or thrusting front kick is a useful self-defence tool provided it is not used higher than your own waist (unless you are very skilful). The legs are much stronger than the arms and terrific power can be applied, especially to the groin and knees of an attacker.

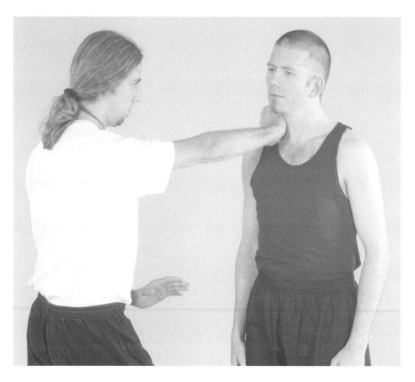

Chop or knife hand strike.

Low side thrust kick.

BELOW: Snapping or thrusting heel kick.

BELOW RIGHT: Shin kick with toes.

Groin kick with toes.

Knee to groin.

Knee to ribs.

Shin kick: Provided you are wearing stout shoes, low fast kicks to an attacker's shin can keep him at a distance, weaken his leg and set him up for other strikes; it's also very painful!

Toe kick to the groin: A classic self-defence move, this technique is better applied with the toes of a stout pair of shoes than the instep (though the instep might be a better bet if you're wearing sandals or flimsy footwear). Against a male, the foot can be raked back as well as kicked up, which can be very debilitating, **even fatal**.

Knee to the groin: Another classic move, this technique can be very effective at close range, particularly when combined with a palm heel strike. Most people are aware of this vulnerability and will take steps to protect their groin unless distracted or

Armpit area.

Kidney area.

caught off guard (also applies to kicking the groin). **Potentially dangerous.**

Knee to the ribs: Although shown here in a rather flamboyant move (not so in keeping with a self-defence technique), kneeing the ribs can be very effective if your attacker stumbles or bends down for some reason. The knee has the same mechanical advantage as the elbow, but is even more powerful due to the bigger muscles driving it, and can penetrate all but the thickest clothing The ribs at the sides usually have little muscle protection except in some very well-developed bodybuilders. NB The patella, or kneecap, is susceptible to damage. Use the top and bottom of the knee only.

Other occasionally vulnerable areas: The armpits, kidneys, base of the skull, and the backs of the knees can also make good targets under the right conditions and if the right weapon is employed. **Note:** strikes to the base of the skull can be fatal.

Base of the skull.

Instep kick to back of the knee.

Low side thrust kick to back of the knee.

The armpits are usually not available unless the attacker is wearing light shirt or T-shirt, but they have little muscle protection and can be vulnerable to a gouging attack or penetrating attack such as a toe kick.

The kidneys are another area that is often hidden by thick clothing, but if they do become available, elbow, knee, hammer-fist or palm heel strikes can cause injury if strongly applied.

If the back of the head becomes an available target the base of the skull is a very vulnerable area to a hammer-fist blow.

If you get behind your attacker, kicking hard through the back of the knee with plenty of penetration and follow-through will generally bring him to the floor, usually with a painful landing on his knees. Another technique that can be applied is to jump with both feet landing in the backs of the attacker's knees, holding onto their body to keep your balance. Few people could remain upright if even a relatively small person jumped on them in this way and the added weight would cause greater damage to the knees.

Finally, all the body's joints: elbow, knee, fingers, ankles, even toes are vulnerable targets if exposed.

Philosophical Studies

Some time ago I had the opportunity to train with some fellow Tai Chi Chuan practitioners, all of whom had been involved with the art for many years. We all approached Tai Chi Chuan from different perspectives, some of us more martial, some more health or aesthetically orientated. During one session one of the participants observed that when I spoke about practising Tai Chi Chuan I referred to it as training, whereas when many of the other participants referred to it as study. They were noting more than a semantic difference. I have always firmly believed that the only way to really understand Tai Chi Chuan and even the principle 'Tai Chi' is to train yourself to comprehend it physically. In so doing you come to an intuitive understanding that also permeates the intellect.

Having said that, it is still worthwhile studying some of the related philosophies and texts related to Tai Chi Chuan. Chief amongst these, in no particular order are: the Tao Te Ching, the I-Ching and the Classics of Tai Chi Chuan.

There can be little doubt that the origins of Tai Chi Chuan are Taoist in nature, the Tai Chi symbol itself being part of Taoist philosophy, and both the Tao Te Ching and I-Ching are central tenets of Taoism. The Tao Te Ching is perhaps the easier to comprehend and provides a clearer insight into the understanding behind Taoism. A good tip is to read several different translations to glean an understanding from many perspectives, as translations of the Tao Te Ching vary enormously in their flavour and tone and there are many versions to choose from. The I-Ching is more inscrutable. To truly understand it requires years of study and it is a work that really calls for a teacher. Most people think of the I-Ching as an oracle, a form of divination, but it is far more than that. The symbols that make up the non-verbal content of the book are meant to be a way of depicting and describing the interaction and nature of the universe.

The I-Ching explores the principles of Yin and Yang via the medium of broken and unbroken lines. Broken lines represent Yin and unbroken lines represent Yang. From this we get a binary system where a state is either positive or negative. To further complicate the issue each Yin line can be young Yin, fixed yin, or old Yin, Yin which is moving toward Yang and each

The Tai Chi or Yin Yang symbol.

Yang line can be young Yang, fixed Yang, or old Yang, Yang which is moving toward Yin. Old Yin and old Yang lines are called moving lines. A set of three lines make a trigram and two trigrams make a hexagram. Each hexagram is an image, a kind of cross-sectional snapshot of an aspect of reality or an instant in time; past, present or future. The I-Ching can be used for divination because the order of the lines, together with the changes indicated by any moving lines, indicate a pattern in the flow of events that we call everyday life.

Generally, to use the I-Ching as an oracle, the practitioner will ask a question, either written down or held in the mind, and then use some sort of random system for generating the lines. Popular methods include separating a pile of forty-nine Yarrow stalks to give the number of lines or tossing coins. The Yarrow stalk system is complicated but the coin system revolves around flipping three coins (or one coin three times) for each line. Traditionally, old-style Chinese bronze coins are used. These coins have a hole in the middle (usually square) and an inscription on one side, which is taken to represent Yin, but nothing on the other side, which represents Yang. If all three coins are Yin the line is old Yin, if all three coins are Yang the line is old Yang. Two Yang and one Yin indicate Young Yang, while two Yin lines and one Yang indicate young Yin.

It is said that the postures and techniques possible in Tai Chi Chuan can be described using the trigrams and hexagrams that make up the I-Ching. If this is so, then the sixty-four hexagrams when considered along with all the moving lines give thousands of permutations.

More directly concerned with Tai Chi Chuan are the classics of Tai Chi Chuan. These works were written by Masters of the art and can usually be found in compilations, so you can study them all from one book. Again, try to get hold of several different interpretations and base your understanding on a mixture of them. Try to read and understand the pure translation of the works, as well as the author's interpretation, if you can, and compare it to your practical experience of Tai Chi Chuan, you'll get more out if them if you do. Try not to get too bogged down in reading though, it's no substitute for doing – or not doing (Taoist joke). A selection of lines from the Classics with an author's interpretation appears in Appendix III at the back of this book.

Note

6 The sleeves of traditional Chinese garments were voluminous and contained pockets for carrying small items.

3 Intermediate Level Training in Tai Chi Chuan

Reaching this standard of training in Tai Chi Chuan is no mean feat. If you've worked through to this level you already have quite a profound understanding of Tai Chi Chuan and its disciplines. The next four principles are the bridge between the mundane and the more esoteric practices of Tai Chi Chuan.

The four principles in the Intermediate stage are:

- Change
- Agility
- Sinking
- Three-level coordination.

Change

Paradoxically; change is, perhaps, the one constant thing in our physical universe. I've heard it said that the one certainty in life is death but, in fact, death is just another change of state, whichever way you look at it. Change, however, can be relied upon to occur unceasingly in the physical world. Change is a characteristic of both life and the physical universe.

Many people dislike change. Or at least the idea of change, as change highlights the uncertainty of our existence. This may be a simple survival trait – unknown and changing environments are often hazardous. The truth is that change cannot be avoided. Fighting against change only causes discomfort and stress. From the perspective of Tai Chi Chuan, and Taoism

generally, change is to be welcomed (the worst state to be in is that of stagnation).

Change should neither be sought out unnecessarily nor resisted. If we can embrace change and flow with it we have the opportunity to guide our path and make the most of what each change may bring.

Change is a principle of Tai Chi Chuan for the fairly obvious reason that all movement requires change. If you practise the Form all your life and repeat the movement a million or more times, you will never perform the Form in exactly the same way twice. The differences may be minute but they still exist, just as two snowflakes are never exactly the same, even though countless billions of them have and will exist over the course of time.

Change can be used actively to enhance your training in Tai Chi Chuan. In Taoist and Tai Chi theory, Yin gives rise to Yang and Yang gives rise to Yin in constant progression. So it is that by training in one way the opposite effect can be enhanced.

Slow and Fast

During the elementary level you will have practised the Form slowly and then more slowly still. There comes a point though where it's not possible to slow the Form down any more without the movement falling into disarray. That doesn't mean it's not possible to slow the movement down any more at all, it just means you've reached the limits of your current ability to perform it at that speed. At this point, it's possible to switch to practising the Form fast in order to extend your ability to practise slowly.

Practising fast, while still keeping all the previously learned principles in place, is by no means easy and again you will quickly reach a point where it is not possible for you to practise the movement faster without it falling into disarray. That point will be much slower than you think during your first session of practising the Form fast. When you've settled down to a reasonable speed (at this point if your Form takes you four to six minutes to perform at normal speed you may be able to get it down to three minutes), practise this way for a couple of weeks. Then switch back to practising as slowly as you can and you'll find you can perform the movement more slowly than you could before you did the fast practise. Again there will be a limit to your ability. Stick at this new pace for a couple of weeks and then switch back to fast. Again you should find that your ability to perform fast has increased before reaching the point where you can no longer hold all the principles in place while practising.

By repeating this switch between slow and fast movement several times over a number of months you will greatly improve your movement, at both fast and slow speeds, and eventually you will be able to perform the Form correctly at combat speed.

Extending the Practice

It's possible to incorporate other attributes into this training regime. For instance: you could practise with low and high postures, using low postures to increase your ability to perform with high postures and visa versa. Also large and small movements can be practised and extended in this way.

When you've used the technique to increase your ability in the individual areas you can combine them. Low posture with large movements done slowly verses high postures with small movements done fast.

This training should be done carefully and honestly over a long period of time in order to truly stretch your abilities. It's most important to evaluate yourself carefully so as not to fool yourself that you can practise faster than is really the case (because actually the standard of the other principles in your movement has dropped due to the increased speed, for instance), or indeed to fool yourself that you can practise more slowly than is really the case for similar reasons.

Grasping this principle will enhance all aspects of your movement and although it is the first principle at this level you'll find yourself returning to this technique again and again to improve your Tai Chi Chuan.

Agility

Agility is not a trait that many people would immediately associate with Tai Chi Chuan. This is due more to common perceptions of what agility means than any notion that Tai Chi Chuan is a clumsy art.

When most people think of agility they picture an acrobat, tumbler or perhaps a famous footballer. This kind of agility, though a great skill in itself, isn't particularly relevant to Tai Chi Chuan. In the practice of Tai Chi Chuan, however, it is necessary to develop agility, though of a different calibre.

The kind of agility required in Tai Chi Chuan has more in common with the movements of a mature cat than the athletic tumbling of a kitten. What is required is a sure-footed ease of movement. A practitioner of Tai Chi Chuan should move as though oiled.

The key to agility in Tai Chi Chuan is largely down to correct application of the posture considerations, discussed earlier, correct alignment, correct stepping and correct placement of the body's centre of gravity. This is easy enough to say but how can one achieve these ends?

The first step will be to revisit your training in posture, roundness and coordination. A few weeks focusing on these basic skills at this level will generally lead to an epiphany in the way that Tai Chi Chuan movement works. Follow this by spending a little time ensuring that your stepping and body lightness are up to scratch.

Beyond the skills already trained, enhancing your agility will require the honing of balance and training yourself to step easily, as required, in any situation. A great technique for improving your balance is to practise the Form with your eyes closed. At first, this can be very disorientating; it's surprising how much we rely on our eyes to help balance our bodies. Removing the sense of sight from the equation forces us to use our inner ear (the body's organ of balance) exclusively to remain balanced. Practising this way for several months results in a heightened internal sense of balance, independent of the sense of sight.

Improving your ability to respond with sure-footed stability in any situation is twofold. Firstly, your practice of Push Hands should move on to free stepping, if it hasn't done so already, and you should practise with partners who will stretch your ability if at all possible. Try to maintain stability and balance at all times, while moving easily from posture to posture, even when surprised, and here it will be necessary to introduce fast attacks into your repertoire, if you haven't done so already. Paying attention to posture, coordination and alignment while practising will pay dividends.

The second training technique that will enhance your ability to move with agility is to practise stepping, your Form and even Push Hands on a variety of surfaces in a variety of conditions. If you've only ever practised Tai Chi Chuan on the flat floor of a practice hall, your living room, patio or a nice, even lawn you're in for a surprise.

Different surfaces require more attention to stepping and sometimes even a different approach. On a flat wooden floor you can slide your foot to a new position, skimming just millimetres above the surface. On rough grassland this isn't possible and each step must become more deliberate with the foot lifted well above obstacles. Sand, ice, snow, gravel and surfaces that incline should also be used, when available, to train both your Form and Push Hands. Gradually, combined with your improving balance, an innate agility will develop, improving your Form on any surface and giving you a distinct advantage in sparring and combat situations.

A word of caution: increase the difficulty of the surfaces you train on gradually and be comfortable on them with the Form before you attempt Push Hands training. It's easy to twist an ankle on uneven ground and falls are more likely (make sure your breakfalls are up to scratch).

Sung and Chen – Relaxing and Sinking

It is said that Chen cannot be studied without Sung and, in truth, Sung cannot be truly attained without Chen. Sinking and relaxing are intrinsically linked. Sinking is an important principle to grasp in Tai Chi Chuan. It is from sinking that a practitioner becomes rooted and it is from the root that power and stability come.

Master Lam used to advise: 'Sink all your weight below your knees'. Of course it's not physically possible to bring all the body's weight to below the knees but by relaxing away tension in the upper body and having correct posture and alignment it can feel as though that is indeed the case.

The Tai Chi Chuan Classics speak of storing energy and then releasing that energy 'like an arrow from a bow'. Sinking is the method required to store energy and relaxation of the joints and muscles allows that energy to be discharged, unhindered, when required.

Relaxing of the joints and muscles while releasing energy is what is referred to in the Tai Chi Chuan Classics as 'passing the thread through the nine crooked pathways' and refers to Jin travelling up from the root of the kidney meridian in the sole of the foot, joining with Jin from the Tan Tien expelled by the action of the diaphragm and passing through the spine, joints and muscles unhindered to the palms or fingertips.

Sinking requires two elements. Directing the Chi to the Tan Tien and the physical relaxation of the upper body combined with good posture and alignment. Directing the Chi to the Tan Tien is largely an internal task, requiring a focus on the Tan Tien and deep, low abdominal breathing. Relaxing the upper body requires a physical effort and the correct attitude of mind.

To many people, saying that relaxation requires effort is contradictory but this is because they are thinking of relaxation in a non-Tai Chi Chuan way. Sung is more than simply slumping down and switching off. The character Sung depicts long hair that is allowed to hang loose, rather than being tightly braided. But hair in good condition has body, it can be styled into a shape that it will hold unless conditions become extreme or it is restyled.

To relax properly requires the right state of mind, one in which the spirit is maintained in an alert and uplifted manner but in which the mind is serene and untroubled. The Classics recommend that the Chi is sunk to the Tan Tien and the 'Spirit of Vitality' lifted to the crown of the head. Sinking the Chi to the Tan Tien requires that the focus of the mind be on the breathing that should be in the lower abdomen, the conscious awareness should be active and focused on what is taking place, both internally and externally.

When the correct attitude of mind and awareness are in place and the body is held in a soft and flexible manner, rather than floppy or tense, then, provided the posture is correctly aligned the centre of gravity sinks lower and lower as time goes by. If your centre of gravity is low you will be more difficult to unbalance.

Master Lam used to advise: 'Practise the Form as if doing it under deep water'. As you might imagine, practising the Form against the resistance of deep water would require you to be deeply rooted and yet very relaxed, particularly in the upper body, in order that your own movements do not unbalance you.

In fact, it is a very good training method to practise Tai Chi Chuan in water that comes up to the chest. When I was training this principle, I was fortunate enough to live near a swimming-pool which was a consistent four feet in depth throughout its length. It was an old pool and on a Sunday morning, particularly in winter, was often practically empty and was ideal for this sort of training. If you've ever tried to practise Tai Chi Chuan in water you'll know that it is very difficult even to retain contact with the bottom of the pool, let alone practise the movements! It is, however, entirely possible once you find the right method and is an excellent way to learn the true meaning of Sinking and Relaxation – Chen and Sung.

Even without actually standing in water, moving as if submerged by imagining the density of water all around you, will help you to attain the correct balance of soft and hard, floppy and tense, which is the relaxation referred to as Sung. Sung is a state from which both hard and soft can come easily and which should be returned to when hard or soft are not required.

Chen Sung Ching – The Three Firmnesses Coordination

Chen Sung Ching is really a refinement of the practice of Chen and Sung. When a practitioner is at the correct stage of development to practise the Three Firmnesses, it usually takes relatively little work to accomplish this principle. Generally, however, no amount of effort will allow someone who isn't ready to practise it to have much success.

Having developed correct relaxation – Sung and Sinking – Chen, lightness is added to the mix to achieve three focuses in each movement: Sinking, Relaxation and Lifting. When this is achieved you will feel rooted on every step, yet light and mobile at the same time.

This principle is merely the simultaneous application of three abilities already achieved. The best way to hone the skill is by practising the Form and Push Hands, and related exercises, with these things in mind.

When the four principles outlined in this level are achieved, your Tai Chi Chuan should take on a noticeably different quality. By the time you can apply the Three Firmnesses you will begin to be able to

control the forces used, both by others and yourself, during Push Hands or combat much more effectively. Where previously you may have been thrown off balance by your partner's attempt at a technique or by your own attempt to apply a technique, you'll find that a new level of inherent stability and control can be asserted over any given situation.

Ting Jin – Listening to/Sensitivity to Force

Ting means to listen, Jin is force, thus, together, we get listening (to) force. The kind of sensitivity required in Tai Chi Chuan is aptly referred to as listening (even though most of this sensitivity is applied through looking or tactile senses). Listening implies a willingness to focus on another person, to suspend your desire to be heard and to understand the opinions and ideas of the speaker.

The first step when joining with a Push Hands partner, or an opponent in a fight, for an exponent of Tai Chi Chuan is to discern their intent so we can follow their actions with our own.

The fighting strategy of Tai Chi Chuan is unlike any other used in the martial arts, even among other 'Internal styles'. Pa Qua stylists use evasive circular movements to attack the opponent from an angle and/or direction in which the opponent will be weak while the Pa Qua stylist is strong. Xing-I stylists use Jeet (as in Jeet Kune Do), the principle of interception, to attack the opponent strongly at the moment when the opponent attacks, slipping inside the attack to deliver devastating power just at the point when the opponent is extending or retreating. External styles usually have simpler strategies: be faster and beat the opponent to the punch, be stronger and dominate the opponent with strength, be tricky and catch the opponent off guard and so on.

Tai Chi Chuan uses a strategy based on the idea of following the opponent's movement and intention while diverting it to your own ends. To do this the practitioner of Tai Chi Chuan must 'Yield' to the opponent's attack and stick closely to the opponent during the encounter, thereby neutralizing their movement and forcing them into bad posture and broken movement, at which point an appropriate technique can be applied to overcome the opponent.

To apply this strategy we must use sensitivity – in particular we must use the unique kind of sensitivity implied by Ting. To return to our listening analogy, listening is not a passive activity. To listen you must actively engage with the speaker, giving your full attention to what is being said while at the same time focusing on the meaning of the dialogue. When applying Ting we must use our eyes, body and other senses to be aware of subtle, sometimes tiny, changes in the opponent's stance, movement, power and demeanour and interpret those changes correctly in order to Yield and Stick in the right amounts at the appropriate time and also to use the right technique when the moment presents itself.

To become expert in the use of Tai Chi Chuan requires that we become expert in Ting Jin. The only way to cultivate Ting Jin is to practise Push Hands and related exercises assiduously for a long time. For this reason many Tai Chi Chuan exponents take every chance they get to practise Push Hands and match with other people but it is important to focus your efforts correctly if you are to have the desired result. Using sensitivity and yielding to force doesn't require you to give in passively but it does require you to follow the attack or intent of your opponent in order to overcome them, not to lead your own campaign by having a preconceived idea of what you will do or blindly lashing out with a technique in the hope that it will work or, and this sometimes happens to long standing practitioners, rely on an arsenal of well-tried responses that have become ingrained through years of use. While the latter approach can sometimes pass for skill, it's not the true skill required by Tai Chi Chuan and will let you down eventually, especially if you meet someone who is versed in the use of Ting Jin.

When entering into a confrontation, whether with a training partner or an attacker watch for any sign of movement or change of stance. Never look into the eyes of your opponent. A practised fighter can mask their true intention and use their gaze to confuse and unbalance you. Instead fix your gaze lightly at about the base of the throat and use your peripheral vision to watch the opponent's entire body. Don't watch their arms or legs specifically, by the time the weapon is in motion it is often too late to counter it.

Engage the arm or arms of your opponent, if possible, lightly but with sufficient weight so that you're not 'floating' on the surface of the limb. Try to feel for any shift in weight or direction. Once you've connected with them, try not to let go or retreat away from them, move away only in response to the opponent's advance, using Ting Jin to discern exactly how far and how fast to move.

Practising Push Hands and related exercises with your eyes closed can be useful in acquiring Ting Jin as you must rely on the use of the sensitivity of hands and arms to apply the strategy of Tai Chi Chuan. It's more difficult to rely on preconceived attacks or habitual responses when you can't see your opponent.

Related Practice for the Intermediate Section

Experimentation

To a certain extent experimentation characterizes this level of study, exploring the methods used in training to see where and how far they lead. It is important not to get too carried away with experimentation however. Always remember 'all roads don't lead to Rome', contrary to the old saying, and you can seriously derail your training by inventing your own methods without clearing them with your instructor. The key point here is that your instructor has already travelled this road, or at least the bit that you are trying to negotiate, s/he will already have an idea of where the pitfalls are, what are good routes and what 'shortcuts' lead to dead ends. Always seek advice when you want to try something out or 'improve' on a training method.

Having said that, it is important to experiment carefully with the training methods your teacher gives you. This rarely, if ever, involves creating your own methods, but thinking about what the training is trying to achieve and seeking to adapt it to your own abilities and needs is a worthwhile activity.

Free Step Push Hands

At some point during this level of study you will undoubtedly be introduced to free step Push Hands. Fixed step Push Hands is useful because it instils the essentials of Push Hands technique. Not allowing your feet to move, forces you to get to grips with dealing with your opponent's attempts to push you by using good posture, coordination and technique; it also helps to improve your stability. Free step Push Hands helps with the development of Lin (agility) and is more realistic from a combat perspective.

One of the first things to understand about free stepping is that it is not a linear exercise. Sure you can take forward and backward steps but emphasis should be placed on using angles when moving with your opponent. Purely linear stepping is a tendency that, if left unchecked, will lead to the monotonous and entirely unhelpful backward and forward motion witnessed sometimes at Push Hands competitions. Choreographed 'San Shao' type exercises can help to avoid this type of interpretation of free stepping and so can practising with more experienced practitioners who have already avoided the linear trap. The key is to use space freely and in all directions.

Free step Push Hands, white shirt deflects a push.

White shirt pushes back.

White shirt continues to press forward, black shirt steps back.

White shirt steps diagonally in to push.

Black shirt deflects and shifts his weight to his left.

Black shirt steps diagonally right and presses white shirt.

Black shirt steps in and pushes, white shirt deflects.

Technique Sparring

Technique sparring is a little known practice. As the name suggests, this type of sparring is for the practice of technique alone. It is of inestimable value when it comes to discerning appropriate technique, correct fighting distance and good form. Technique sparring is also an excellent medium for experimentation.

Technique sparring is practised slowly, typically at between one-third and half normal combat speed, and without the use of any power whatsoever, the idea being to prevail against your partner with the use of technique alone.

This is a difficult practice to become proficient in. The immediate tendency of most people is to speed up in order not to be caught by a technique that would otherwise have got through. This must be avoided at all costs. In reality, in combat, you would have been moving at, or near, your maximum speed and an extra burst would probably not have been possible. Stopping the attack in this way is self-delusional – you fool yourself into thinking you would have stopped the attack when in reality you would not. The other tendency to afflict the beginner is that of applying power to the slow-moving techniques – not enough to hurt but enough to push a strike through a softly applied and slow-moving deflection. Again this leads to self delusion, you think that your techniques are working when in reality they would have been neutralized.

When you first begin this sort of training it's almost impossible to avoid going too fast or using too much force on occasion. One way to get control over this is to have another student, preferably a more experienced one, or your teacher, watch your bouts, so that they can stop and advise you when you go wrong.

Once you get the hang of this training it is a marvellous medium to practise for combat, as you can try out techniques without worrying about whether or not they will work, and in so doing find out what will work for you.

This type of sparring is not a substitute for Push Hands and other similar training, it is another way to practise and should be used in conjunction with Push Hands to develop rounded technique.

Unlike Push Hands you should start with just the back of your wrists touching at a slightly longer distance than would normally be the case with Push Hands. When you start, anything goes, the only rules being no speed, no power. Once you get the hang of not using speed or power, injuries should be extremely rare but to begin with you should wear groin, shin and hand protection (light sparring mitts) in case of accidents. In fact there's no reason not to continue with these protective items, even when you're experienced, you can never be too careful.

Full-Contact Sparring

Not every practitioner of Tai Chi Chuan will want to engage in full-contact sparring. In fact, it's only the minority of dedicated martial artists who generally wish to pursue the art to its logical conclusion. Not wishing to engage in full-contact bouts is fine and no-one should try to persuade someone who doesn't wish to pursue the martial aspect of the art this far to do so. It's not for everyone.

However, without testing your ability at full speed and power, ideally against a number of different styles, you can never truly say that you have learned to use Tai

Chi Chuan as a martial art. It comes as a shock to most people the first time they are faced with an opponent who is moving fast and applying techniques with power, indeed who is actually trying to attack them in earnest! But it is the only way to prepare yourself for this situation.

Full-contact sparring will not teach you much else, other than what it is like to fight with someone at full speed and power. In fact half a dozen to a dozen or so bouts are all most people need to learn what lessons this practice holds but there is no other way to get this experience, except perhaps to go out and pick fights with strangers (a practice to be advised against most strongly).

Some people will shake their heads and say that this sort of training has no place in the practice of Tai Chi Chuan but they couldn't be more wrong. Masters such as Yang Lu-Chan (founder of the Yang style) and his sons had many contests without rules and accepted challenge matches against other martial artists to demonstrate their art, as did most of the great exponents of the past.

Full-contact sparring is dangerous! There are techniques that should not be employed and it is essential to use safety equipment. While it is necessary to engage in full-contact sparring if you want to become a fully rounded martial artist, it isn't absolutely necessary to risk injury. You're not getting paid for this after all. Advice on the minimum requirements for the practice of full-contact sparring appear in Appendix V at the back of this book.

Never engage in full-contact sparring without your teacher's permission and without at least two other senior people to assist you, one of whom should be qualified in first-aid and resuscitation techniques.

Vital Point Striking and the Use of Special Palm Shapes

It is beyond the scope of this project to go into detail about the use of vital point striking; once again a whole book could be devoted to this topic. Contrary to what some people would have you believe, 'Cavity' or Vital point striking is not fundamental to the art of Tai Chi Chuan, though it is something that any serious martial arts student should study in depth. A brief overview would be useful however.

Traditionally, there are thought to be some 108 vital points on the body that are useful in combat. In actuality many of these are usually inaccessible due to muscular development or heavy clothing. Some thirty or so are generally useful and are invariably quite obvious, located mostly on the neck, head, spine and genital areas or focused on nerve clusters such as the solar plexus. There are techniques to attack the muscle (similar to giving a dead leg), that can incapacitate an attacker, and choke holds that can induce unconsciousness.

More esoterically there are formulas for attacking points at particular times of the day or night designed to cause injury or death due to the body's weakness in a particular area at a particular time. This last section is of dubious credibility and even more dubious efficacy. While it is true that certain organs are weaker at certain times (the heart is more vulnerable in the early hours of the morning due to the fact that it is habituated to slow down during deep sleep for instance), there is no clear evidence that all the other organs are so weakened at particular times. Even if the formulas are correct, trying to remember the complex list of points to strike and at what time of the day would make this practice of little use except, perhaps, to an assassin.

Key to striking vital points is the use of particular palms or hand shapes. Vital points are small and generally need to be struck fairly precisely, so finger and one knuckle strikes are the most appropriate weapons, chiefly the spear hand, phoenix eye fist, emperor fist and kicking with the toes. The spear hand appears in most Tai Chi Chuan forms in such movements as 'High Pat on Horse' and, though the other two fist shapes can be associated with several different strikes, the phoenix eye fist is a natural enhancement of such movements as 'Shoot Tiger with Bow' while the emperor fist can be used with the 'Step up to form Seven Stars' sequence. These examples are from the Yang system but once the fist shapes and targets are understood it soon becomes clear which techniques could be used with them.

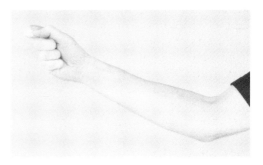

The Phoenix Eye Fist.

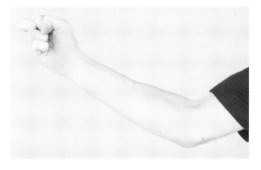

The Emperor Fist.

Phoenix Eye Fist used with Shoot Tiger with Bow.

The Spear Hand – correct alignment.

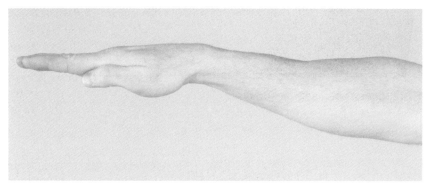

Emperor Fist used with Seven Stars, first punch.

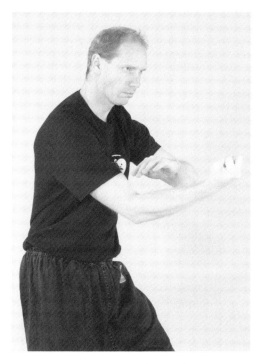

Emperor Fist used with Seven Stars, second punch.

Some would argue that the fist shapes are more important than the vital points themselves. It's very difficult to hit vital points accurately while engaged in combat but the application of a strike where all the force is focused on a very small area to almost any part of the body can have a devastating effect. A punch that can easily be absorbed by someone with well-developed abdominal muscles when delivered with the whole fist will often drop the person when the fist is turned into the phoenix eye. Of course if the above principle is applied to an already vulnerable point, the effect is multiplied considerably.

It goes almost without saying that such techniques can be extremely dangerous, both to use and to train, and great care should be taken in practising with them to avoid injury. The use of these techniques for self-defence should only be as a last resort when life and limb are threatened as they can result in the death or permanent disability of those on whom they are used.

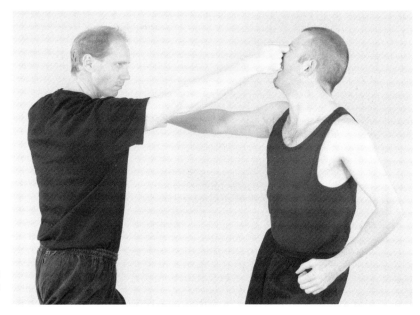

An application of the Phoenix Eye Fist.

LEFT AND BELOW: Two applications of the Emperor Fist.

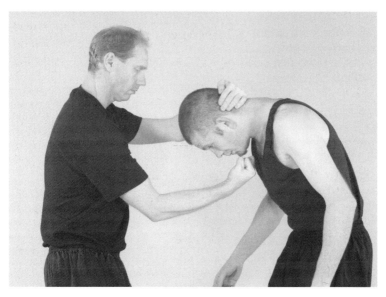

Bag Training

Bag training is yet another area of which many practitioners of Tai Chi Chuan would not approve but again this is mostly due to the perception of bag training that most people have. The kind of training that boxers do on punch bags is of little use to practitioners of Tai Chi Chuan, except perhaps as a supplementary aerobic exercise.

Tai Chi Chuan does contain punches however and to punch with the knuckles requires a certain amount of training, if not conditioning, of the hands. Using the knuckles to strike anything but a soft area of the body will cause most people, who haven't trained their fists, to be injured more than the person they have struck. For many people even striking tensed muscles with the fist would result in a sprained if not broken wrist. Heavy hanging bags and wall-mounted bags are the ideal way to train the correct alignment of the fist when striking and also to build up the strength of the muscles and tendons in the hand and wrist.

The type of bag used should be well stuffed with rags, so that it forms a solid but yielding mass. Thin leather gloves of the kind found in gardening shops are ideal for bag training, much better in fact than padded bag gloves. This is because they allow a better formation of the fist and because, in fact, padding will only serve to slow down the strengthening of muscle tissue and tendons. Gloves are necessary to stop chafing of the skin on the bag.

Practice should be undertaken carefully. It's best to start softly and slowly and build up, paying particular attention to the alignment of the wrist and hands. Initially, concentrate on developing the strength and alignment of the technique as you gradually increase the power and speed. Once you can punch the bag hard and fast without any ill effects, try incorporating whole body movement combined with Sung Jin into the technique so that even more power is delivered to the bag. Avoid skipping around punching at different angles and speeds as would a boxer, if you really want do this sort of training, focus mitts worn by a partner are a better bet in any case. Wall-mounted bags are generally better for the purposes of Tai Chi Chuan than a hanging bag, though initially a hanging bag is more forgiving.

When developing the phoenix eye fist, or spear hand, though much of the above holds true, more care must be taken to avoid injury. A better way to start conditioning these hand shapes is to stand just a little more than an arm's length from a wall-mounted bag, make the hand shape

with both hands at arm's length and allow yourself to fall forward onto the fingers or knuckles (taking great care to keep the alignment correct and the hand shape strong). Lower yourself forward until your face is level with the bag then thrust yourself back using the hand shape. As the strength in your hands and wrists improves, increase the starting distance from the bag so that your weight adds more force to the technique. When you have developed great strength in a hand shape you can try using just the one hand to support yourself (keep your legs spread wide, two shoulder widths at least, while working with single hands), again start at just over an arm's length and work up to greater distances slowly. Only when you've developed the hand shape strongly by this method should you attempt to practice punching the bag.

Upright position – Phoenix Eye training.

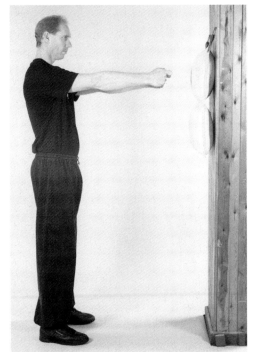

TOP LEFT: Contacting the bag – Phoenix Eye training.

ABOVE: Lowering to the bag – Phoenix Eye training.

LEFT: Upright position – Phoenix Eye training.

In order to actually use strikes done with the fists or hand shapes, bag training of some kind is most desirable, otherwise the first time you realize that your hands are not strong enough to deliver a technique could be when you hear an ominous cracking sound when you strike something solid.

Upright position – Spear Hand training.

Contacting the bag – Spear Hand training.

Lowering to the bag – Spear Hand training.

Upright position – Spear Hand training.

Studying Anatomy and Physiology

Traditionally, Chinese martial arts have always been closely associated with Chinese medicine and many famous martial artists were, and are, also respected physicians. There is good reason for this. Understanding what makes the body work is a valuable tool in disabling it, and conversely understanding how to damage the body can help in the understanding necessary to repair it.

If you're really serious about Tai Chi Chuan as a martial art or wish to learn about Chinese medicine as well, it's well worth studying both the Chinese and Western approach to anatomy and physiology. Though the understanding of anatomy doesn't differ markedly between Chinese and Western thought, there are some differing views on what makes it all tick. A study of the theory of meridians and the five elements is essential if you want to understand how the Chinese approach to physiology works. Any good book on Western physiology will impart the essentials of how the scientific mind perceives the workings of the human body. Chief systems to study from a martial arts perspective are the nervous, circulatory, respiratory and digestive.

Anatomically the alignment and rotation of bones and the distribution and placement of muscles, nerve clusters, organs and major arteries are all important to the martial artist.

Tips on Throwing

Sensei Shioda, a pupil of O Sensei Ueshiba the founder of Aikido, once stated that combat is 70 per cent strikes and 30 per cent throws but training is 70 per cent throws and 30 per cent strikes. This is because throwing techniques require much more practice in order to be effective than do strikes, even though more strikes are used while actually fighting.

This disparity of effort to effect may seem unbalanced but it must be remembered that one correctly executed throw will generally end a fight, since once the opponent is on the floor you usually have complete control of the situation, even if the throw has not disabled them; whereas, it will often take several correctly executed strikes to subdue an opponent.

Throwing techniques should not be thought of as a 'soft option', great injury may be occasioned by a throwing technique, particularly if the person being thrown does not know how to fall correctly. It's tempting to labour the point again but please reread the section on breakfalls – enough said!

There are basically two approaches to throwing an opponent; close body throws, such as are seen used in Judo, where the opponent's body is levered by the thrower's body and 'out-body' throws, seen in Aikido, where joint locks and unbalancing techniques are used to throw the opponent. Throwing techniques in Tai Chi Chuan are mostly of the out-body type.

Classically speaking, in order to throw an opponent you must first uproot them. So far, so good, but how do you go about uprooting someone? It helps to first think about what makes someone rooted in the first place. As we've seen already, rooting is a combination of correct posture, sinking and relaxation. In order to uproot someone therefore we have to remove one or more of these qualities from our opponent. All the classical principles of Push Hands come into play; yielding to the opponent can cause them to become unbalanced and lose their posture, sticking closely can cause the opponent to become tense and unable to sink their weight; in either instance it will become easier to throw them off balance.

Redirection in Throwing Techniques

In practical terms there are a few things that can make throwing techniques more effective and easier to apply. The first is redirection. Redirection can be said to have two levels of operation. At its simplest it may be just a matter of distracting the opponent's attention prior to applying the throw, techniques such as slapping the opponent's face or feinting a finger strike to the eyes will cause most people to 'jump' losing their focus for a fraction of a second, this generally has the effect of uprooting them, either through a loss of posture or because they become stiff and cannot properly sink their weight. It's generally easier to apply a light, fast slap or feint than it is to land a strike with power. Ideal targets are the face, eyes and groin.

Black shirt slips in and uproots white shirt.

Black shirt redirecting white shirt's attention with a fast slap.

Black shirt takes white shirt down.

Black shirt redirects white shirt's force upward, uprooting.

Black shirt applies Jin in a downward action.

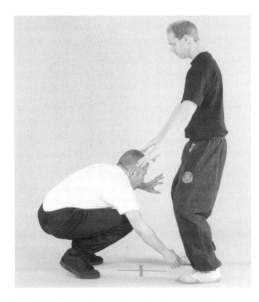

White shirt is forced to the floor, off balance.

There is part of a verse in the Tao Te Ching:

> That which shrinks
> must first expand.
> That which fails
> must first be strong.
> That which is to be cast down
> must first be raised up.

This stanza alludes to a more sophisticated type of redirection. If you want to throw someone down you must first lift them up slightly, if you want to throw someone to the left you must first push them to the right. A good illustration of this is a technique from the opening sequence of the Yang style long form (also appearing in Wu, Sun and other styles of Tai Chi Chuan) where the arms are raised to deflect the incoming arms of an opponent upward, tending to lift the opponent slightly, before being pressed down causing the opponent to be thrown down.

Black shirt redirects white shirt's force upward, uprooting.

Black shirt steps away, creating space.

This technique can be extended so that the opponent is then raised up again (perhaps at an angle) before being thrown down heavily.

Making Space in Throwing Techniques

Another important principle applied to throwing techniques is that of 'making space'. To make a throw effective, or in some cases more effective, it is necessary to make space for the opponent to fall into. Many people try to execute throwing techniques without causing the opponent to extend; this either causes the throw not to work because the opponent can regain their balance or else the throw turns into a

Black shirt pulls white shirt into the void.

White shirt prepares to attack.

ABOVE: White shirt is flipped over and thrown down.

Black shirt rolls back using 'Grasp Birds Tails' to catch the fist.

Black shirt steps to the side, applying a bent wrist lock.

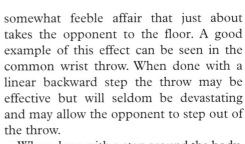

White shirt is flipped onto the floor.

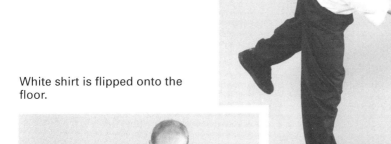

somewhat feeble affair that just about takes the opponent to the floor. A good example of this effect can be seen in the common wrist throw. When done with a linear backward step the throw may be effective but will seldom be devastating and may allow the opponent to step out of the throw.

When done with a step around the body, creating much more space for the opponent to fall into, the effect of the throw is magnified greatly and is much more difficult to escape from.

All throwing techniques rely heavily on correct timing. Try to throw the opponent too soon and you'll end up having to lift their weight or use a lot of localized strength just to throw them at all. Leave the throw too late and the opponent will

Black shirt rolls back using 'Grasp Birds Tails' to catch the fist.

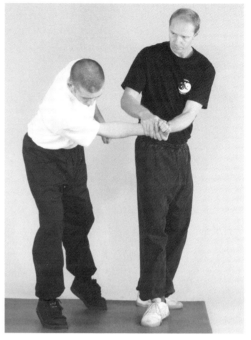

Black shirt steps right round, applying a bent wrist lock.

White shirt is thrown up high due to the extra space created.

Still flying!

adjust their stance and position so that they are no longer uprooted, again you'll have to use localized strength in order to effect any kind of throw. If the timing is correct however your opponent will be thrown without effort and any force you apply to the execution of the throw will make the effect of the throw more devastating. Developing correct timing comes back to sensitivity, trained in Push Hands, and joining with the opponent. Both Push Hands and Tai Chi Wrestling, described earlier, are ideal methods of practising these skills.

Chan Ssu Jin – Silk Reeling Force

Chan Ssu Jin is usually associated with Chen-style Tai Chi Chuan, though there is no reason why the technique should not be employed by any style of Tai Chi Chuan.

Chan Ssu Jin is often referred to as spiral energy and it can be employed in both attack and defence. Chan Ssu Jin is both a technique of movement and a type of Jin or intrinsic energy generated through the movement of the body. Done well, seemingly tiny movements can throw an attacker off balance, both while attacking and being attacked. There are many refinements of Chan Ssu Jin practice, only the basic exercises are covered here. If you wish to develop this practice, and it isn't part of the syllabus of the class you attend, there are many good books and videos on the subject.

Acquiring the intrinsic energy associated with Chan Ssu Jin is a task for your Nei kung practice but the application of Chan Ssu Jin also requires a particular spiral motion of the body when dealing with

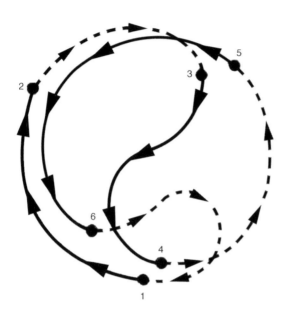

Right-hand pattern for
practising the Chan Ssu Jin.

the opponent's force. The traditional way to practise this motion is to stand in a forward stance and trace a shape similar to the shape of the Tai Chi symbol in the air with the fingers. The key to success in this endeavour is to use the body to move your arm and only turn the hand at the wrist in order to allow it to follow the shape.

The best way to begin the practice is to draw the Tai Chi symbol shown on page 89 about 30in (75cm) in diameter on a large piece of paper, making the outline bold. Hang the drawing up at chest level about 6ft (2m) away then practise the movements outlined below, taking care to develop the movement from the movement of your body generated by the waist, not the arm and hand.

There are two kinds of silk reeling practice, natural silk reeling and reverse silk reeling. Natural silk reeling requires the palm to be turning upward, rotating from the inside to the outside. Reverse silk reeling requires the palm to be turning

downward, rotating from the outside to the inside.

Natural silk reeling techniques refine the use of 'Peng Jin' or ward-off energy that can be used to deflect an attack or 'bounce' the opponent away. Reverse silk reeling techniques, refine the use of 'Lu Jin' or roll-off energy that can be used to neutralize an incoming force.

Single-Hand Practice

If using the right hand, stand in a forward stance with 60 per cent of your body weight on the front foot, observe the posture considerations outlined in the section on Roundness. The hand pattern starts at point 1 on the above diagram for the right hand, travelling round the circles in the direction of the arrows. The solid lines equate to the hand positions in natural silk reeling and the dashed lines equate to the hand positions in reverse silk reeling. During the natural silk reeling phases the palm is gently turning upward,

Left-hand pattern for
practising the Chan Ssu Jin.

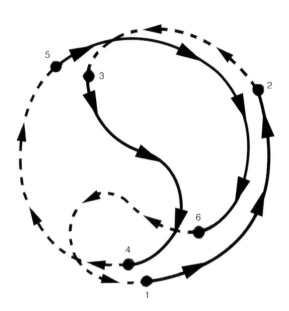

rotating from inside to outside, while during the reverse silk reeling phases the palm is gently turning downward, rotating from outside to inside.

Try to follow the pattern of lines accurately. Remain relaxed. Start with big circles done slowly and smoothly and gradually reduce the size. Take your time, allow yourself to get familiar with the feel of the pattern. Coordinate your movement with the rotation of the Tan Tien and, above all, make sure that it is your body that moves your arm and not just your arm moving on its own. Balance your practice by becoming familiar with the movement on both the right and left sides of the body. Focus on rooting through the feet and amplifying the power of the legs through the waist as you turn from the Tan Tien.

Once you've grasped the feel of the movement, it's possible to practise faster and to try smaller circles, internalizing the movement; but don't be in a hurry to do this. Even when you're used to the movement it's a good idea to practise the circles at both large and small sizes as both are useful in combat. Continue to repeat the movements for some time, ten to twenty minutes while learning the technique. It is the repetitive nature of the movements that helps instil the rhythm of silk reeling in the body.

Silk reeling energy can be used to draw the opponent into emptiness, neutralizing their efforts, to bounce the opponent away, using their own energy against them, and to generate Fa Jin, attacking force, that strikes suddenly at the opponent.

As well as singly, the hand patterns can be practised together and a forward/backward motion can be added. Stepping drills can also be used to help you become familiar with the interaction of stepping with the movement.

4 Advanced Level Training in Tai Chi Chuan

The Chinese term Si Gung is usually translated into English as Master, and Sifu is used to refer to an accomplished teacher. However the English word Master carries with it connotations that the term Si Gung does not. In English the word Master can be used to refer to a teacher, such as a Maths Master or English Master but it can also imply someone who has 'mastered an art', that is, someone who has reached a point in their study of that art where everything that can be known or done in the art is known and can be done. In truth, there are very few things in life where this state of mastery would be possible, nevertheless this is the state that springs to mind for most people when someone is introduced as a Master of a martial art. Few martial arts could be mastered in this way and Tai Chi Chuan certainly cannot. In truth the furthest one can go in the practice of Tai Chi Chuan is to become an advanced student, as there is no end to the potential for learning and refinement.

The term Sifu may be bestowed by a teacher or organization on an individual to show that they are an accomplished teacher. The term Master is more usually bestowed by the general consensus of opinion among others in the martial arts community as a mark of respect for an exceptional teacher or to denote the head teacher of a particular school or family. Of course one advanced student may be much more advanced than another advanced student, particularly if they have trained for many more years!

To some, the fact that total mastery of the art of Tai Chi Chuan is not really feasible may be seen as a disincentive but this all depends on your point of view. The fact that Tai Chi Chuan can be endlessly refined and improved upon is simply due to the fact that it is such a deep and profound art, which means that there is the possibility of endlessly discovering new facets and intricacies in its practice and of continuing self-discovery.

An advanced student of Tai Chi Chuan is one who can correct mistakes that creep into their Form or application based on their understanding of the principles of Tai Chi Chuan and can therefore continue to improve their art without constant recourse to a teacher. That doesn't mean that such a person would never consult their teacher or another teacher for guidance, rather it means that if no such person is available, refinement and improvement is still possible. Once all the principles are understood and internalized, it's possible to continue on your own if you must.

The four principles in the Advanced stage are:

- Yin and Yang (separating and embracing empty and solid)
- Tai Chi Kung (transforming Tai Chi Chuan into Tai Chi Kung)
- Lien Jin Hwa Shen (the refinement of Jin into Shen [spirit])

• Hsu Jing (seeing the void or finding the tiger amongst the corn).

Yin and Yang (Separating and Embracing Empty and Solid)

The first principle of the advanced stage of Tai Chi Chuan practice is actually the one major principle of Tai Chi Chuan. As the principle of Change characterizes intermediate level training in Tai Chi Chuan so the refinement of understanding of empty and solid characterizes the advanced level practice of Tai Chi Chuan.

All the training undertaken to reach this point has involved refining the way you move and execute techniques in Tai Chi Chuan but, in essence, all those refinements have been facets of the study of Yin and Yang, empty and solid. By now your movement and understanding of Tai Chi Chuan should be at the stage where you are beginning to see and feel movements as having empty and solid or soft and hard components.

Each posture in the Form shapes the body into empty and solid components. This composition of empty and solid is relative. For example, the right hand may be considered solid in comparison to the left hand but empty when compared to the left leg in a particular movement. Furthermore, the fingers may be considered solid when compared to the palm of the same hand or vice versa depending on the application of the movement.

At any given time, any part of the body and the body as a whole can be separated into Yin and Yang or empty and solid. If we take the movement Brush Knee and Twist Step done with the right leg forward, for example, the left hand and right leg can be said to be solid while the right hand and left leg are empty.

Brush Knee showing some distribution of empty and solid (darker areas are more solid).

This can be applied to each movement at each moment in the form and using the principle of Yin and Yang, it is possible to trace the movement of empty and solid through each posture and each change of posture throughout the form. Understanding this principle properly will help you to eradicate double weighting from your postures (see Appendix III).

The principle can be further subdivided. In the example given above the heel of the

119

right foot would be solid while the ball of the right foot would be empty and the reverse would be true for the left foot. The right leg could be said to be 60 per cent solid and 40 per cent empty, the left 60 per cent empty and 40 per cent solid. These subdivisions can go on and on. The idea, though, is to be aware of the interplay of empty and solid throughout the movement and it is not necessary, or desirable, to over-intellectualize the process. If you know what is empty and solid in yourself it is easier to distinguish empty and solid in someone else and this is important for the application of techniques in Tai Chi Chuan.

The Tai Chi Sphere

There is a line in the Tai Chi Classics that states: 'Let no part of the body have gaps, let no part cave in or out. Permit no discontinuity in movement.' This statement is the basis of the concept of the Tai Chi Sphere. If all parts of the body are rounded, yet not over-extended, and all parts of the body form a cohesive whole, without defect or incline, and all movement flows continuously, without break or hindrance, it's as if the practitioner is moving within a giant sphere whose centre is rooted in the Tan Tien. Forces applied are effortlessly redirected, as if thrown off by a giant spinning top, and power applied by the practitioner has an inertia that seems to roll over an opponent.

Another pertinent observation from traditional Tai Chi lore is that it is easier to leave a (spinning) circle than to enter it, as anyone who has tried to get on a fast spinning roundabout in a children's playground will confirm. If you can make yourself the centre of such a continuous and constantly turning sphere it's hard for an opponent to apply techniques and easy for you to exert force.

The development of the Tai Chi Sphere is a direct consequence of refining the movement of Tai Chi Chuan with the understanding of empty and solid or Yin and Yang, both in the practice of the Form and in Push Hands and related exercises. In the practice of the Form, focus on the feeling of the flow of weight from one side or part of the body to the other, the centre of gravity constantly acting through the solid leg, as one technique evolves into or gives way to another. For example, in the movement 'Step Back to Repulse Monkey' in the Yang-style Long Form, one hand is extended, palm up, in the act of catching the opponent's wrist. As the body's weight is transferred from one foot to the other and the grasping hand sweeps down and then up on the other side of the body, the hand goes from Old Yin to Young Yang to Old Yang to Young Yin as the weight is transferred onto the hand, turned by the body and then swept back. The feeling is as if water were flowing in a network of pipes within the body, slopping its weight from one side to the other smoothly, as only a fluid can.

In the practice of Push Hands and related exercises, a conscious effort should be made to discern the feeling of empty and solid, both in yourself and your partner. When receiving energy, in the form of a push or strike, try to follow the flow of empty and solid. Doing so will give you new insight into the appropriate amount to yield and stick and will help you to neutralize your partner, if discerned correctly.

By training the Form and Push Hands from the point of view of feeling and understanding Yin and Yang, empty and solid, in the movement, all other principles and considerations can be absorbed and understood and a new freedom of movement can be attained. Ultimately, only the understanding of Yin and Yang is important, although it may take many years of training and practice before this begins to become the reality of your experience. Constant re-evaluation of the other principles will be necessary in order to achieve this transformation of focus.

Tai Chi Kung

When the practice of Tai Chi Chuan becomes internalized, Tai Chi Chuan itself can become a form of Chi Kung or energy work. For this to be the case the Form must be practised in harmony with the principles of Tai Chi Chuan and thus conform to the principle of Yin and Yang, or Tai Chi, itself. To achieve this, the six external coordinations, covered in Chapter 2 (Continuity – coordination) must coordinate with the four inner coordinations.

By now you should be fully conversant with the six outer coordinations. To recap, the inner coordinations are:

The Shen [Spirit] must coordinate with the mind: the inner spirit of vitality, the essence of consciousness, must be aligned with the Intent of the mind.

Mind must coordinate with Jin: the Intent of the mind must be aligned with the refined intrinsic energy of the body.

Jin must coordinate with Li (strength): the refined, intrinsic energy of the body must be applied harmoniously with and aligned with the body's physical movement.

The inner [Shen, Mind, Jin] must coordinate with the outer [first six principles].

Shen translates as spirit. In the martial arts you could say fighting spirit, the indefin-

able presence that is ourselves (more on Shen a little later). This inner essence must be coordinated with the Intent of the mind, 'I' (pronounced Yee) so that our spirit and mental focus can work as one.

I – Intent

The principle 'I' is perhaps one of the most difficult to comprehend for many people. 'I' translates roughly as intent which gives rise to much of the misunderstanding associated with the term. To English speakers, intent is simply the decision to do something and although this is a component of 'I', it doesn't adequately describe the process of applying it. Many people make the logical, though incorrect, assumption that 'I' is another word for willpower or mind-over-matter.

It is said in the classics of Tai Chi Chuan: 'The body follows the Chi, the Chi follows 'I' (sometimes written as the mind).' Clearly what is being referred to here is something other than the process of thinking or a simple decision on the part of the individual to do something. The intent referred to in Tai Chi Chuan is actually a product of awareness.

Awareness is a function of mind more intuitive than the concentration that most people would describe mental processes as. Concentration, as the very name implies, directs the mind to a single point to the exclusion of everything else. If you're concentrating very hard on something, people can speak to you and remain unheard, you will be unaware of them or anything else that's going on around you. Awareness, on the other hand, is encompassing. If you develop your awareness, the minutiae of situations and circumstances are often apparent without effort. Many people will turn round if you stare at them from behind or from one side, even though they couldn't possibly have seen you. If asked why they turned around they will either say they don't know, they just felt the urge to, or they will say they felt that someone was looking at them. Some people seem naturally more aware than others.

Awareness can be enhanced and developed, particularly by the Nei Kung and similar techniques. It is a calm open state of mind, where the faculties are fully engaged but unfixed on an individual task or process. By it's very nature, awareness is not concentrated but it can be focused, a gentle process of applying the same state of mind to a particular goal or aspiration. It is from the focus of awareness that we derive 'I' or Intent. When attempting to apply Jin to a technique at the precise moment it is called for, judged by our sensitivity, we must be fully aware of what it is we are doing and what we want to do. This is not the same as concentrating on the actions we are taking, that tends to lock the mind and inhibit the use of Jin. When Intent is used the focus of awareness is gentle, pervasive and continuous, it is the overall action, including the result that is important, not the individual steps needed to attain the result. This state of mind is conducive to the application of Jin and allows the whole body, physical, mental and spiritual, to come into play during the delivery of the technique.

The intent of mind 'I' must be coordinated with the Jin, the refined whole body force associated with the internal martial arts. When 'I' is applied, Jin may follow that application. Jin is unlike the use of strength. It is the sudden releasing of power rather than exertion of power by muscles; like the releasing of an elastic band or a bowstring that already has potential energy that only has to be let go of in order to take effect.

Jin must coordinate with Li (physical movement). Without a correctly aligned body, moving in the correct way, Jin cannot be released. If the body is not moving as a unit or is stiff and awkward then Jin will be blocked and only localized muscular power will be present. Jin and Li must be delivered together using Sung Jin (relaxed force, described earlier). If Jin is released before Li it will be of little effect, if Li precedes Jin only local muscular force will be present.

Finally, these inner coordinations must be coordinated with the six outer coordinations so that the whole being – Body, Mind and Spirit – are unified in the application of Tai Chi Chuan. When this is the case throughout your Form, Tai Chi Chuan will have become Tai Chi Kung and though still a fixed set of postures it will become fresh and vibrant on each execution, never the same twice but an expression of your own coordination and understanding.

The Refinement of Jin into Shen

The last two topics of the advanced section are esoteric and increasingly difficult to put into words.

As stated earlier, Shen is spirit – martial spirit, spiritual essence, the root of personality. Shen can be expanded, strengthened and grown or allowed to shrivel and dissipate. It is perhaps not the divine but it may be linked to the divine more directly than other parts of our being.

There is a Nei Kung practice associated with this topic but this must be learned directly from a teacher and is beyond the scope of this book.

However, there is more to the transformation of Jin into Shen than Nei Kung techniques alone, no matter how advanced they may be. This practice is also about our direction and focus as a human being.

After all, spirit is, ultimately, what makes us what we are. In order to accomplish the transformation of Jin into Shen we must take responsibility for our lives and refine all of ourselves, mental, physical and emotional into spirit.

In order to cultivate Shen we must become the 'Superior Man' (not excluding women here, this is a reference to a repeating theme in the I-Ching). The Superior Man is a state of consciousness where action is right. Not right or wrong, as in a moral decision, but right as in entirely appropriate for the circumstances we find ourselves in. Somewhat akin to a high state of Push Hands or combat, where the appropriate response is what works effortlessly, not some technically correct movement that is a struggle to perform.

One approach that probably has its roots in the early Taoists' understanding of the place of martial arts in society, is to discern the correct course of action based on our perceived awareness of any given situation, weighed against our life's experience, or perhaps we could say our understanding of the Tao. As stated earlier, many Taoist hermits were ex-soldiers (finishing one's days as a hermit on a quest for spiritual fulfilment was a common enough retirement plan). For a soldier, martial arts are a part of life and the sense of focus and discipline inherent in the martial arts complements a life of spiritual dedication and discipline. While a soldier, moral questions are answered by circumstance – for example, we kill the enemy because those are our orders and to obey our orders is our duty. As a civilian, no such clear-cut course of action exists. To become a pacifist (at least in the Western sense where fighting is refrained from at all costs, even at the cost of our lives or the lives of loved ones) is to deny part of our nature, the instinct to survive. To do that is to separate ourselves from the Tao.

It should perhaps be borne in mind that until relatively recently, Chinese martial arts were much more weapons-orientated than they are today. Swords, spears and a variety of other weapons would have accounted for somewhere between 70 and 90 per cent of a martial artist's training (as opposed to 10 to 20 per cent of the average modern martial artist's practice) and challenges or duals, whether with weapons or without, could easily end in the death of one, or both, of the combatants. Moreover, living a hermit's lifestyle could expose those seeking spiritual fulfilment to attacks from bandits, who often occupied the same remote areas and who also invariably used weapons while making raids. Hermits and monks were not seen as easy targets as they were usually highly skilled in the martial arts and would often do far more damage to any bandits foolhardy enough to attack them than would be done to them.

The solution to the moral dilemma, presented by the need to bear arms and fight to the death, for the Taoist spiritual seeker is right action, becoming the Superior Man. To accomplish this, some sort of code of conduct is required but not one restricted to arbitrary rules of behaviour that could never be flexible enough to be part of the Taoist's way of life. The code of conduct required places two obligations on us; firstly, we are bound to be as conscious as possible of all the factors in our lives and the situation we find ourselves in and, secondly, to act, or not act, in accordance with what we know to be right action, based on the our awareness of the world, our place in it, our understanding of the situation, our experience of life and our intuition – in short, our understanding of the Tao.

Of course there will be times when we find that, with hindsight, we could have acted differently and perhaps should have, in our own estimation at least, based on our new evaluation. Hindsight is 20 × 20. However, if we acted genuinely, in accordance with our best understanding at the time, we should be serene in the knowledge that what we did, or didn't do, was all we could do. After all, in the greater scheme of things we can never know what is ultimately the 'right' thing to do; indeed human concepts of right and wrong are irrelevant in the cosmic sense. All we can do is what we genuinely believe to be the right action at the time.

Living up to this code is a lot more difficult than it looks. Firstly, who can say that they are always as conscious as possible in every situation, taking the trouble to be mindful of all factors and weighing them diligently against their understanding? And even when we are conscious and aware of all consequences, how often do we have the courage, conviction and the wisdom to follow the course of action we feel we should, whatever the cost?

The real difficulties are that our own lack of insight often blinds us to the subtleties of life and the situations we find ourselves in, and our enslavement to our baser emotions (anger, desire, jealousy, attachment and so on) prevent us from being true to ourselves and to this, or any other, code of conduct. The only answer is the constant refinement of our spirit – doing our best to be the 'Superior Man'.

The benefits of following this code of behaviour are more than just a feeling of being at peace with our actions. The more we are able to be conscious in every aspect of our lives, the more of our lives are truly lived in our spirit. This enhanced strength of spirit can add a new dimension to our practice of Tai Chi Chuan. Master Lam used to say 'everything is a feeling'. Ultimately there is no difference between body, mind and spirit. The goal of this practice is to develop continuous awareness, maintaining awareness at all times, so that all action is conscious action, focused by the 'I', governed by the whole spirit.

Hsu Jing (Finding the Tiger Among the Corn)

The final principle of the advanced section is, possibly as you might expect, the most subtle and difficult to attain.

It is said that, Tai Chi is rooted in Wu Chi and further that, Wu Chi never leaves Tai Chi. Wu Chi is the primordial, the pre-existing, potentiality, stillness, the void. Tai Chi is duality, complementary opposites, the root of everything in this physical universe.

From the perspective of Tai Chi Chuan you could say that Wu Chi is stillness while Tai Chi is motion, or that Tai Chi appears when there is motion. Yet stillness precedes motion, is always present in motion and is returned to when motion ceases. If we took a glass cylinder and poured in some blue-coloured water followed by some red-coloured oil then, provided the liquids were at rest, they would remain separated, as oil floats on water. This is analogous to the state of pure Tai Chi, Yin and Yang are separate because they exist but they are in a still state and so are not intermingled. Stirring the two liquids will cause them to mix. The more vigorously they are stirred, the greater the degree of mixing that takes place until it is difficult to see the separate red and blue liquids at all, just a magenta one. Stop stirring and the liquids will slowly separate out until they are once more entirely distinguishable. In other words, the faster the motion the more Yin and Yang combine, the slower the motion the more they separate, this understanding has a direct bearing on the application of Tai Chi Chuan techniques.

It's harder still to see the stillness in motion. The best example is the turning point at the centre of a spinning disk. If we have a spinning disk of solid material, then the closer to the edge of the disk we get the faster will be the speed of rotation. As we move closer to the centre the speed of rotation slows down. Theoretically somewhere at the precise centre of the disk is a point of stillness, though this may well be on a sub-atomic level. Theoretically in Tai Chi Chuan motion is derived from stillness and in practice the more we can slow our minds the more time there appears to be. When applying Tai Chi Chuan if your mind is calm and unhurried even fast action appears less frantic, the more you become caught up in the activity the faster the action appears to be and the more difficult it is to keep on top of it.

On a practical level there is an advantage in seeking the source of an action. For instance, if you try to intercept a fast punch by deflecting it at the wrist your chances of success are low. This is because the fist is the fastest moving part of the arm and trying to intercept it close to yourself means that your own arm is closer to your centre and therefore slower. If you extend your arm and intercept the opponent's arm closer to the elbow you capitalize on the rotation speed of your own body while cutting down the relative speed, and therefore power, of the incoming arm.

These examples are crude and on a physical level but, unfortunately, they will have to do, as it's not possible to give examples on more subtle levels. Hopefully they will suffice to convey something of the nature of the relationship between stillness and movement because that is what this principle is all about – that is, finding Yin within Yang and Yang within Yin. Find the still point in any action and you have control of that action, by going to the source of the movement.

Finding the still point, the turning point, is very difficult to do, hence the expression 'finding the tiger among the corn'. Tigers, being well camouflaged for hiding amongst long dry grasses, would be invisible to the casual observer, especially when keeping still. Even in stealthy movement they would be hard to spot. Seeing Yin within Yang or stillness in movement requires a refinement of awareness that is one of the supreme accomplishments of the art of Tai Chi Chuan. This seeing is of an intuitive nature. It is a function of our awareness and sensitivity, honed by years of dedicated training. This intuition isn't confined to seeing stillness in motion. It can be applied to solid and empty, Yielding and Sticking, in fact all the complementary opposites that make up Tai Chi Chuan.

Related Topics for the Advanced Level

Tung Jin – Understanding Force

On a practical level, possibly the highest attainment in Tai Chi Chuan is Tung Jin. Tung Jin is the final refinement of Ting Jin (listening to/sensitivity to force). When the nature of force is understood, the highest skills of Tai Chi Chuan can be honed. The only way to achieve this understanding is to constantly refine sensitivity and awareness, because Tung Jin is an intuitive understanding, born out of practical insights gained in the practice of Push Hands and related exercises, in combat and throughout all training in Tai Chi Chuan. It is of course possible to come to an intellectual understanding of force but this would be of little use in the practice of Tai Chi Chuan.

To achieve a state of Tung Jin, training in Tai Chi Chuan, and specifically in Push Hands and related exercises, must be approached in the right way. There are of course different phases of training; when you first start, the focus will be mostly on attaining and keeping the correct posture, later this will give way to concentration on techniques from the Form, at some point, coordination of movement will be the primary goal, in order to put power in the techniques, and the application of strategy will be important also. There are many facets to good practice in such exercises and throughout the book we've touched on a number of them.

Push Hands and Combat

There follows some final advice on this subject that may help to put it all in perspective. At this point it may be useful to look at Push Hands and combat as separate things (which indeed they always are) and from the point of view of what may be wrong or missing in our practice so the following advice is in the form of a discussion on observed failings, with advice on their possible rectification.

Sticking to the Principles and Strategy of Tai Chi Chuan

Probably the most common reason for lack of skill in Push Hands, or combat for that matter, in those who have practised Tai Chi Chuan for many years is not adhering to the principles of Tai Chi Chuan. This stems sometimes from a lack of understanding but more often from the abandonment of the principles under pressure. Many capable practitioners, who demonstrate fine Forms and good Push Hands technique with their peers, lose their ability in combat or when practising

with an unfamiliar partner. In this, they demonstrate their lack of faith in the principles of Tai Chi Chuan, in that they resort to some other method when the going gets tough. In my experience the principles of Tai Chi Chuan are peerless. There is no better method for engaging an adversary, whether in practice or actual combat.

The most common manifestation of this lack of faith is 'Double Weighting' which manifests itself as meeting force with force or not yielding. This comes about in two ways: firstly in the tendency to resist the attempts of the opponent to apply this or that technique by pushing back against the direction of their attack and secondly by attempting to force your own attack to work, even though it has been anticipated and resisted by the opponent.

The reason for the above error is usually incorrect attitude in training, particularly in Push Hands practice. Again, as with so many things, there are two, apparently opposite, causes. The first mistake is the tendency to treat Push Hands practice as a battle or a real fight. It is neither! The root of this mistake is usually ego, the desire to win or to prove your skills superior to those of your opponent. Push Hands is an exercise. It is meant to be the training ground for the key words (Listen [sensitivity], Yield, Stick, Neutralize, Control/Attack [Issue Force]). If you treat it as a contest it will be difficult to develop the sensitivity necessary to discern the appropriate moment to apply the rest of the strategy and the tendency to resort to physical traits, such as speed, strength or trickery will become rooted in your subconscious. As mentioned earlier, Master Lam used to say 'If you practise this way (wrongly), even if you win, you lose!'. You lose because ultimately you will train yourself into bad habits and not acquire real skill.

The second reason for this lack of faith in the principles of Tai Chi Chuan is also rooted in the practice of Push Hands. Some people, perhaps having misunderstood the message of the advice in the previous paragraph, practise Push Hands as if it were a dance, with neither partner attempting to discern the correct moment to yield, stick or issue force. Simply moving in the pattern of Push Hands without attempting to apply the strategy or principles achieves little and does not prepare the practitioner to apply those principles when called upon to do so.

The best approach to the practice of Push Hands is to attempt to apply the principles to the best of your ability while not caring whether you overcome your opponent or are yourself overcome. Either way you learn something; If you do manage to apply the strategy and principles and overcome your opponent you will see what you are doing right, if you are overcome by your opponent you will learn what you are doing wrong and ultimately how to correct it. Even if your opponent practises incorrectly and overcomes you by superior physical abilities, eventually you will discover how to deal with those abilities by using the principles of Tai Chi Chuan. You still benefit!

The Use of Force in Combat or Push Hands
These days there is much talk of 'Fa Jin' (lit. attacking energy) and the use of internal or intrinsic power. While it is true that Tai Chi Chuan, Chi Kung and other internal arts develop power by conditioning the body from within and developing the ability to issue energy directly from the whole body, rather than relying on external physical conditioning, it is not the case that this ability entirely replaces physical activity or can be used completely without physical effort.

The myth that Masters of Tai Chi Chuan can merely point at an individual or place a palm on them and send them hurtling away stems, almost certainly, from the observation of a Master performing a technique with excellent application of force and impeccable timing, due to great sensitivity. Someone highly skilled in Tai Chi Chuan will often be able to put an opponent off balance simply by changing direction unexpectedly or subtly redirecting their attack, leaving themselves in a strong rooted stance and their opponent almost falling over, particularly if their opponent is a lot less experienced. At this point placing a finger or two on the unbalanced person and applying a small amount of force can send them flying. It may even be possible to send them sprawling by suddenly advancing or moving a hand as if to strike them, as their own reaction would be likely to send them flying in their off balance condition. This is no trick! It is a demonstration of Tung Jin at a very advanced level. The application of strategy and the principles being displayed are extremely subtle.

Conversely there have been demonstrations given where a practitioner has simply pointed at an individual, invariably one of their students, and the person has fallen down or leapt back as if pushed. Such demonstrations do more to demonstrate the suggestibility of some individuals than to show any skill in Tai Chi Chuan. There are many stage hypnotists who can send people flying about in this manner by the use of hypnotic suggestion alone, often without any long-winded hypnotic preamble, who have never studied a martial art!

The advantage of internal power over physical strength is a subtle one. It is not that internal power is necessarily more powerful than physical strength, it is rather that it can be applied without committing the momentum of the body to the technique. A good analogy would be to compare internal power with a very sharp knife and physical strength with an iron bar. Either of these, used as a weapon, could kill you but I would rather face someone armed with an iron bar than someone armed with a very sharp knife (if that someone also knew how to wield the knife), the reason being that an iron bar, once swung, is set on its course; the harder it is swung the more fixed its course is and it only has the power to hurt or kill if it is swung hard. Despite its power, it is possible to evade it and defeat the attacker. A sharp knife in the hands of an experienced attacker, on the other hand, is light, manoeuvrable and hard to predict and it only has to touch you to cause damage. Internal power allows the practitioner to issue energy without much physical commitment because it is 'soft' and subtle in its approach, like the use of a very sharp knife. Its superiority over physical strength lies in this, not in the amount of power that can be generated.

There is a line in the Classics attributed to Wang Zongyue that is usually translated as 'No excess, no insufficiency'. Though, in fact, this is the first four characters of an eight character line. The other four characters translate as 'Expand as your opponent contracts' and the opposite may be inferred 'Contract as your opponent expands'. The importance of this when issuing force is in two parts. 'No excess, no insufficiency' implies using just enough force to accomplish the desired technique and no more. Most people seem to believe that if enough force is good then more must be better. Nothing could be further from the truth! Using Internal power this way (with excessive force) commits the practitioner, physically, to the technique and externalizes the movement, turning

the very sharp knife into a very blunt one; it therefore has all the disadvantages of the iron bar with none of the advantages! Of course, enough force must be used to accomplish the technique and therefore, for techniques to work, they must be appropriate and timed to perfection. This is something that can only be accomplished with great sensitivity and strict adherence to the principles of Tai Chi Chuan.

The second part 'Expand as your opponent contracts' refers to the ability to Stick closely to your opponent. Sticking is a difficult ability to master and, like much of Tai Chi Chuan principle, is often misunderstood. It could further be said that as your opponent contracts, or retreats from you, you must continue to advance, giving no room for your opponent to mount a counter attack (it is most important not to overextend or Yang becomes Yin and your advantage will be lost). Similarly, Contract as your opponent expands is about Sticking as much as it is about Yielding. It infers that as your opponent expands, or advances, you must continue to contract, or retreat, giving no room for your opponent to press home their attack. It is vital, at this point, not to break with the opponent but to stick as close while retreating as when advancing (this is an example of seeing the existence of Sticking within Yielding). The above need not imply linear movement but should also be applied to circular and angular movement. Mastering these principles will make your techniques seem effortless and give you control over yourself and the situation.

Neutralizing
The Classics of Tai Chi Chuan say that 'Energy should be issued like an arrow from a bow', yet how often do we see practitioners of Tai Chi Chuan, particularly in

Push Hands competitions, struggling to push an opponent? This is because they have either not understood how to Neutralize an opponent or how to tell when the opponent is Neutralized.

To Neutralize an opponent means to place the opponent in a disadvantageous position – that is to say, one which is uprooted, off-balance or strategically inferior (or some combination of all three). This is done by the simultaneous application of Yielding and Sticking or, from the Classics, 'Adhering to, joining with and sticking to every movement with no letting go and no resistance.' When this is done the opponent is overwhelmed without effort and cannot help but fall into bad posture and broken movement. At that moment by issuing energy, joined with the energy of the opponent, in a sudden burst, the opponent is sent flying away with only a small visible movement.

To discern the moment when the opponent is Neutralized requires sensitivity that can only be gained by many, many hours of practice in Push Hands and related activities, but it is important to know what to look for in the first place. If, at the point of contact with your opponent, you feel a sense of heaviness, your opponent is not Neutralized and you should not attempt to issue energy. This should not be taken to mean that you feel the opponent pushing back. If this is the case, you can issue energy in the direction they are pushing to great effect, but rather a heavy rooted feeling. When the point of contact feels light, however, you should issue energy instantly. Again, this should not be taken to mean a light contact, this may be due to circumstances and not be an indication that the opponent is Neutralized, but rather be a feeling of lightness or uprootedness in your opponent. When this is achieved the point of contact needs no further attention.

Energy should be issued from the whole body, from the feet up. The Intent, 'I', should be placed in the direction in which the energy is to be issued and beyond the actual target or target area. It is only necessary to focus on releasing energy not on the point of contact; to focus on the point of contact will tend to make the movement external and retard the issuing of force.

Mental Attitude in Push Hands and Combat

The final observation concerns the difference in mental attitude between the practice of Push Hands and combat. In Push Hands, it is not necessary to win and it does not matter if you lose. Practice should be undertaken with a calm mind, a strong Intent and an eagerness to improve in the spirit of discovery. In combat, on the other hand, it may not always be possible to win but it is important not to lose, or at least not to lose badly, if at all possible. Combat should be undertaken with a calm mind, a strong Intent and a cautious and yet, when the time is ripe, decisive manner.

Whereas in Push Hands practice we may try an unlikely technique to see what happens or restrain ourselves when overcoming an opponent, so as not to cause harm, in combat we must stick like glue to the principles of Tai Chi Chuan, have a free and uncluttered mind but do nothing rash or unguarded. And, when the opportunity arises, defeat the opponent resoundingly. A practitioner of the internal arts should fight with a serious mind and a light heart.

Final Words

Hopefully this book will have helped to put some perspective on training in Tai Chi Chuan and will therefore help you make better use of other resources. Whole books could be, and have been, devoted to some of the topics raised within these pages but knowing their place in the scheme of things should help make such works more useful.

Ultimately, there is no substitute for the help and advice of an experienced teacher. Quite apart from teaching you new things, it is vital to have someone who can look at your Form, test your Push Hands and correct your mistakes and misconceptions, especially in the early years of your training.

Most important of all, work within your limitations and develop a passion and enjoyment for your training in Tai Chi Chuan. Without an enjoyment of the Form and practice it's hard to imagine anyone continuing for the many years that it takes to achieve something really worthwhile.

Standing

Rooted in earth, open to heaven.
Empty bridge between worlds.
Life, *ROARS!*

Appendices

Appendix I – Warm-Up and Stretching Exercises

It is helpful to 'warm up' for 5 minutes or so before practising these exercises, good ways to do this include the use of an exercise bike or rowing machine or just running on the spot or skipping.

Circle Knees: Keep the feet together, bend the knees, rest the hands gently on the knees (do not press down with the hands). Circle the knees to the full extent of movement available ten to twenty times in one direction then repeat the exercise in the other direction. This exercise helps to stretch and tone the ankles and knees.

Squat Down: Keep the feet together and squat down. If possible, keep your hands on your hips but if you don't have sufficient flexibility in the ankles and hips extend your arms in front of you to help with balance. For some people it may be necessary to squat only part of the way down until the ankles and hips loosen up. Repeat twenty to thirty times. This exercise increases flexibility in the ankles, hips and lower back.

Circle Knees – starting position.

Circle Knees – to the left.

Circle Knees – back through the centre.

Circle Knees – to the right.

Squat Down position.

Knee Pull-Ups: Lift the right leg and grasp under the foot with your left hand, bring the right arm round and cradle the right knee pulling up, hold for ten to fifteen seconds. Keep the back and supporting leg straight throughout the exercise.

Repeat the exercise with each leg alternately about ten times each. This exercise increases flexibility in the hips and lower back and stretches the tendons in the upper thighs and the buttock muscles. It also helps to improve the balance.

Knee Pull-Up – left side.

Knee Pull-Up – right side.

Bow Stretch – left side.

Bow Stretch – right side.

The Bow Stretch: Place the feet approximately two shoulder widths apart and, keeping both feet flat on the floor, squat down on one leg, keep the other leg straight. Keep the back as straight as possible and lean your hands toward the straight leg. Practise on both sides repeating six to ten times. This exercise stretches the tendons and muscles on the underside of the thighs and calves, it also increase flexibility in the lower back and ankles.

Hamstring Stretch: Place the feet approximately two shoulder widths apart and, keeping the right foot flat on the floor, squat on the right leg allowing the toes of the left foot to lift, reach out and touch or grasp the toes of the left foot, hold for ten to fifteen seconds. Practise on both sides repeating six to ten times. As the name implies this exercise stretches the hamstrings, it also increases flexibility in the ankles and lower back.

Bend back circle arms round and down: Place the feet approximately two shoulder widths apart and, keeping both feet flat on the floor, raise the right arm up over the head, bending back as it passes over the skull, follow with the left arm and when you reach the extent of travel swivel to the right, bringing the right arm and then up until it points vertically into the air. At the same time bring the left arm down so that it touches the right foot.

Hamstring Stretch – left side.

Hamstring Stretch – right side.

Bend back, circle arms
round and down – 1.

Bend back, circle arms
round and down – 2.

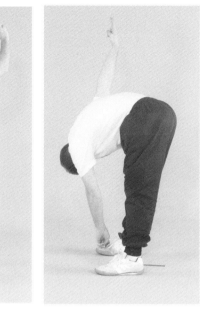

Bend back, circle arms
round and down – 3.

Bend back, circle arms
round and down – 4.

Bend back, circle arms
round and down – 5.

Bend back, circle arms
round and down – 6.

Circle Arms – starting position.

Circle Arms – raise arms.

Circle Arms – turn palms out.

Keep looking at the right hand throughout the exercise until it is pointing vertically upwards, then switch to the left hand and repeat the exercise on the other side. This exercise increases flexibility in the hips, lower, mid and upper back, shoulders and neck.

Circle Arms: Stand with the feet one shoulder width apart, breathe naturally from the Tan Tien. Gently raise both arms in front of the body, palms facing you as you breathe in until they are above your head. Turn the palms out and allow your arms to gently fall on either side of your body as you breathe out. Continue to rotate the arms slowly in this fashion about thirty times. This exercise increases flexibility in the shoulders and arms and helps to calm the mind and body after the previous exercises.

Circle Arms – lower arms to the sides.

135

Circle Arms – begin next circle.

Appendix II – The Pa Tuan Jin

Pa Tuan Jin (lit. eight silk forces) exercises are a form of circulation practice and are a type of the Chi Kung. In all these exercises, it is important to keep the tongue placed behind the teeth and breathe from the Tan Tien. It is the difference between the stretching and relaxing elements of each Pa Tuan Chin exercise that stimulates the circulation, so it is important to stretch as much as possible (without tensing) and then relax as much as possible in each exercise, if you are to receive maximum benefit. For this reason it is best to take an extra breath between each stretching phase of an exercise in order to ensure proper relaxation, especially when you first start these exercises. Repeat each exercise eight times (one time is an in and out breath cycle).

Two hands support the sky: Bring your hands up to the top of your head, palm up,

FAR LEFT: Two hands support the sky – relax.

LEFT: Two hands support the sky – stretch.

breathe in and relax. Stretch up as you breathe out and at the same time rise up onto the balls of your feet and try to keep the palms as flat as possible. When you've let all your breath out, sink back down onto the soles of your feet as you breathe in and lower you hands back to the top of your head. Take another breath out and in before repeating the stretch. (This exercise is always done first in the set of eight.)

NB If you suffer from high blood pressure it is best not to rise up onto the balls of the feet during this exercise.

Stretch down to grasp the toes: Place your feet one shoulder width apart, breathe in and relax. As you breathe out reach down and grasp the toes, let your head relax (don't try to keep looking forward). It is not necessary to have the knees locked back as in traditional Western toe-touching exercises. Pull down with the toes and up with the fingers pushing the knees back a little at the same time as you expel the rest of the air from your lungs. When you've let all your breath out, let go of your toes and rise up as you breathe in.

Shoot bow on both sides: Place your feet two shoulder widths apart, bend your knees slightly, bring your arms up in front of you in a relaxed circle, palms facing you and breathe in. As you breathe out pull one arm back as if drawing a bow string (do not let the elbow move back past the line of your body), extend the other arm with the index finger pointing straight up and the other fingers curled down toward the palm, look through your index finger as if sighting an arrow. When you have let out all your breath bring the arms back in to the relaxed circle in front of your body breathing in. Repeat on alternate sides.

Stretch down to grasp the toes – relax.

Stretch down to grasp the toes – stretch.

Shoot bow on both sides – relax.

Shoot bow on both sides – stretch left.

Shoot bow on both sides – stretch right.

Holding up a single hand: Place your feet one shoulder width apart, breathe in and relax. Raise one hand above your head, palm up, fingers pointing in (similar to two hands support the sky but using just one hand), at the same time press down with the other hand, fingers pointing forward, palm flat. Breathe out while stretching. When you've expelled all the air from your lungs breathe in and relax, returning the hands to the resting position.

Shake water from ear: Place your feet two shoulder widths apart, bend your knees slightly and place your palms gently on your knees, breathe in and relax. As you breathe out, let your upper body fall to one side (keep the back straight, don't loll forward) and shake the hips as if trying to shake water out of your ears. Do not move the head by using the neck muscles but

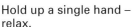

Hold up a single hand – relax.

Hold up a single hand – stretch up right.

Hold up a single hand – stretch up left.

keep it relaxed and it will nod naturally when you get the hip movement right. When all the air is expelled from your lungs come back to an upright position, breathe in and relax. Do all repetitions on one side then swap to the other side for best results.

Twist body: Place your feet one shoulder width apart and stand naturally. Breathe in and relax. Rotate your body around its own axis, keeping the back straight, as you breathe out. If you've turned to the right, turn until you can look at your left heel. When you've expelled all the air from your lungs breathe in and return to the starting position; don't forget to relax. Do this exercise on alternate sides, making sure you take an extra breath between exhala-

tions, both to aid relaxation and to avoid dizziness due to turning the head too fast.

Forward punching: Place your feet two shoulder widths apart and bend the knees slightly. Bring your hands up to your hips, palm up, and curl them into loose fists, breathe in and relax. Extend the right arm as you breathe out, turning the fist over and tipping the knuckles down slightly toward the end of the punch. At the same time, pull back with the left elbow so that the upper body turns but try to avoid turning the hips. To increase vitality and vigour glare fiercely while punching. When you have expelled all the air from your lungs return to the starting position as you breathe in and relax (if you included the glaring technique also relax your eyes and

Shake water from ear – left side, hips right.

Shake water from ear – left side, hips left.

Shake water from ear – right side, hips left.

Shake water from ear – right side, hips right.

Twist body – relax.

Twist body – twist left.

Twist body – twist right.

Forward punching – relax.

Forward punching – right punch.

Forward punching – left punch.

FAR LEFT: Shake body to relieve all ills – relax.

LEFT: Shake body to relieve all ills – bounce.

even close them if you wish). Repeat the exercise on alternate sides. Do not clench the fists tightly during this exercise.

Shake body to relieve all ills: Place your feet together with the backs of your hands, curled into loose fists, resting behind your back just under your ribs, breathe in and relax. As you breathe out arch your body back slightly and shake it up and down using the calf muscles, keep shaking until all the air is expelled from your lungs then return to the starting position and continue to relax. Repeat eight times. This exercise is always done last as it calms and centres all systems. It also differs from the other exercises as there is less emphasis on stretching and more on relaxing.

Appendix III – Excerpts from the Classics

There follows, in no particular order, some lines from the Classics of Tai Chi Chuan that I am particularly fond of, followed by a brief analysis of their meaning. This section is neither definitive nor exhaustive and, as stated earlier, it's advisable to read and re-read as many translations and commentaries on the Classics of Tai Chi Chuan as you can, in order to refine your understanding.

The Thirteen Postures – also sometimes referred to as the eight powers or palms and the five steps or directions. (Not to be confused with the Posture Considerations that form part of the physical principles of Tai Chi Chuan.)

The 13 Postures are: Peng (ward-off), An (push), Lu (roll-back), Chi (press), Tsai (pull-down), Lieh (split), Chou (elbow stroke), Kao (shoulder stroke), Chin (advance [stick]), Tui (retreat [yield]), Ku (look [circle] left), Pan (look [circle] right) and Ting (central equilibrium-centring/rooting [sensitivity]).

'In ward-off, roll-back, press and push you must find the real technique. If upper and lower are coordinated, the opponent will not be able to advance.'

The movements of ward-off, roll-back, press and push, are the cardinal movements of Tai Chi Chuan technique. Pull-down, split, elbow stroke and shoulder stroke form the bridging movements that complete the circle. Advance, retreat, look left, gaze right and central equilibrium refer to the tactics of Yield, Stick, circular movement and Centring/Rooting. A firm foundation in the above will ensure the highest technique, however, one should always start with and return to the cardinal movements, then the opponent will not be able to find an advantage.

'When the opponent is hard and I am soft, this is called Tui (Yielding). When I follow harmoniously and the opponent is forced to retreat, this is called Chan (Sticking).'

Yielding to force while sticking closely to every movement is the essence of push hands. Both the amount of force and its direction must be correctly discerned and Yielding and Sticking must be applied simultaneously if the strategy is to have the desired effect. In order to do this we must acquire Ting Jin (listening [to] force), the ability to sense both the actions and the intentions of our opponents. When the strategy is applied successfully the opponent is neutralized, that is to say, forced into broken posture and awkward movement.

'If the opponent moves quickly I must respond quickly; if the opponent moves slowly, then I respond slowly.'

In the so-called 'Hard Style' martial arts, it is usually believed that being faster and stronger than your opponent is the secret of success (beating the opponent to the punch). Soft stylists do not subscribe to this belief. That is not to say that it is not important to be able to move quickly or that power has no use. Rather, that timing is the key to the successful application of technique not physical attributes. When engaging an opponent we must match the speed of the attack with the speed of our defence because it is only by following the opponent that we can yield and stick effectively and neutralize the opponent.

'If pressured on the left, empty the left; if pressured on the right, empty the right.'

Wherever power is applied should be emptied. If you push on my left shoulder I will not resist but will allow the shoulder to retreat with your push, at the same time I will apply the energy I have taken from my left shoulder to the other side of my body (typically my right shoulder) and bring the force of your push back to you from a different angle. If this is done simultaneously, and the body's integrity is maintained, great power can be derived from this principle. This is using the opponent's strength against them.

'The body is like a wheel; the waist is the axle.'

When the body turns like a wheel and the waist is made the axle, good posture is maintained. This is because the axle shaft keeps the body straight and rooted to the ground. If you can be centred and rooted yet remain flexible and free to turn in any direction you can meet any attack without resistance yet will never be thrown off balance.

'Looking up, I seem ever higher. Looking down, I seem ever deeper. Advancing, I am ever further away. Retreating, I am ever closer.'

The meaning of this statement is to lead your opponent into emptiness. That is to say, when your opponent advances you should follow without resistance until the force is spent; this causes the opponent to overextend and thus become uprooted or double weighted. When the opponent attempts to retreat, you stick close and follow so that s/he is crowded by your adherence to their every movement and s/he is thrown into disarray. Straight line movement should be avoided, whether in advance or retreat.

'Sticking is Yielding. Yielding is Sticking.'
and
'When advancing I advance, when retreating I also advance. When every step advances; then you are without peer under heaven.'

Within Yang there is Yin, within Yin there is Yang. They are mutually dependant, one cannot exist without the other. Therefore, when Sticking some small part should still be Yielding and when Yielding some small part should be Sticking. When this is truly the case, both states are always simultaneously existent and can become one another in an instant.

Yielding and sticking must take place simultaneously for neutralizing to take place. Therefore, if when retreating you still advance your cause and can bring down an opponent as effectively while retreating as while advancing, your skills will be peerless.

'A feather cannot be added, a fly cannot alight.'

Imagine a set of weighing scales with two pans, so perfectly balanced that any force, no matter how small, will set it in motion. When you are centred and rooted yet completely relaxed it is possible, by using great sensitivity to be able to react to even the smallest force so that it cannot overcome you. In the Tao Te Ching, there is a line that says 'the arrow can find no place to land, the rhinoceros no place to thrust its horn'. When you reach this state it is referred to as Tung Jin (understanding force). Your opponent should not be able to make use of your force whether attacking you or being attacked by you.

'People do not know me. I alone know others.'

When you accomplish Tung Jin, the 'I', Intent, of your opponent is always obvious to you and you can discern the strength, direction and nature of any attack at the moment it is launched. At the same time, your own intent is hidden from your opponent who is caught unawares by your movement.

'In appearance the hawk catches the rabbit, actually the cat catches the rat.'

If you have ever seen these two natural hunters in action you may intuitively understand this reference. When a hawk dives on a rabbit the rabbit has no chance to respond, it has not even seen the hawk and is destroyed utterly by the power of the attack. A cat stalking a rat appears altogether different, the cat is absolutely focused on the rat, every sense is tuned to maximum, every muscle in the cat's body is ready to pounce, yet it does not move until the rat moves. Though the cat has the advantage you never feel that it is a foregone conclusion, and indeed sometimes the rat gets away. When applying the strategy of soft boxing a great fighter will appear to wipe out opponents without effort, as if they have no chance at the outset (like the hawk catching the rabbit), but actually the process is much more like the cat catching the rat. The great boxer will wait, aware of every nuance of motion and stillness and, at the optimum moment, apply just what is needed to overcome the opponent.

Above all, avoid the error of double weightedness, to fall into the trap of double weightedness leads to stagnation and confusion.'

On a practical level double weightedness manifests in three ways:

1. Placing the weight of the body on both feet equally or on both hands equally or on both sides of the body equally.
2. Meeting the opponent's force with your own force.
3. Trying to make your own attack work even though it has been observed and resisted by an opponent.

Though this is undoubtedly an oversimplification, it is nonetheless true. It is like trying to press down on both pedals of a push-bike at the same time you expend a lot of effort but go nowhere.

Yang Lu-Chan is reported to have said: 'When you see a practitioner of Tai Chi Chuan who has practised for many years but is still regularly overcome in combat it is because he has not understood the fault of double weighting'.

Not to understand and eradicate the fault of double weighting is the single biggest mistake a practitioner of Tai Chi Chuan can make. One can practise for a lifetime but if double weightedness remains, true skill will always evade us.

'Allow no breaks or deficiencies; allow no hollows or projections.'
and
'When your practice is most refined, even the smallest place is circular.'

When the above is maintained, the practitioner has attained the Tai Chi Sphere, achieving a kind of dynamic stability from which any attack can be thrown off or redirected. This state can only be attained when the boxer is centred and rooted and movement is completely coordinated without any tenseness, awkwardness or hesitation, thus allowing no dent in the smoothness of the circle, neither in nor out – even the smallest movement is rooted in circularity, every facet of your movement is circular.

'Yin does not depart from Yang; Yang does not depart from Yin. This is giving up yourself and following others. But many people mistakenly avoid the near and seek the far.'

Giving up yourself and following others means to have no preconceived plan but to respond instinctively to the opponent through sensitivity. Mistakenly giving up the near and seeking the far means to misinterpret the first sentence by trying to second-guess the opponent. Trying to anticipate the opponent's attack puts us right back to the point of a preconceived plan. The only way to give up yourself and follow the opponent is by applying sensitivity while maintaining your root and centre.

'In order to issue power, you must sink and relax and place your Intent in one direction.'

Power in Tai Chi Chuan is issued from the ground up. Only by having a strong root, good posture and coordination can this be achieved. However, tenseness in the musculature and the tendency to rise up when issuing power will dissipate your efforts. It is therefore vital to sink as power is applied and to relax the body so as not to interfere with the transfer of energy.

'Energy should be issued like an arrow from a bow.'

Unless all our energy is focused in one direction, as stated in the previous lines, this cannot be achieved. This is much more subtle than it at first appears. If the coccyx is not aligned correctly, for instance, energy will be lost because the body is not aligned in one direction. If the whole body does not move as a unit, that is, is not fully coordinated, all the body's energy will not be available at the same moment. If you do not sink and relax there will be no storing up of energy, either your own or your opponent's, and if there is no storing of energy, like the pulling back of the bow string, how can energy be released like an arrow?

'Neither let go nor resist.'

One of the most difficult skills to master in boxing is the art of bridging. Bridging is the term applied to making contact with and joining with the opponent. It is important because, if not done correctly, we are vulnerable as we attempt to cross the bridge. This vulnerability stems from the point of interception Jeet (as in Bruce Lee's Jeet Kune Do [Way of the Intercepting Fist]). At the point of advancing or retreating there is a moment when the body is fixed and open. This is caused by our application of movement into the opponent's field of reach. The internal boxer overcomes this by letting go of his/her own agenda and joining with that of the opponent. Bridging, therefore, is something that happens naturally and the disadvantage is negated. Once the bridge has been crossed it is highly desirable that the bridged state is maintained, hence neither letting go nor resisting, as either would break the bridge and we would have to start again. Like having a tiger by the tail, resistance is futile, letting go is suicide.

'To enter the gate and be guided on the path requires instruction. If you practise your art without cease, then you can cultivate correct methods on your own.'

When starting off in the martial arts, guidance and instruction are necessary. After much practice and when the inner principles of the art have been understood and internalized, it is possible to continue training on your own and still improve your art. This is because you can judge your technique and movement against your understanding of the principles and any errors that creep in can be eradicated.

This is a very dangerous statement for some people to hear! Until you have really understood and internalized these principles, guidance and instruction are most definitely needed. Yet many people hearing this will conclude at some point that they are in a position to continue their training without further recourse to their teacher. Unfortunately, it is very easy to fool oneself into thinking that all the principles have been understood when in fact one has only just scratched the surface of the art. Traditionally, it is the teacher who informs the student when he or she is ready to strike out on their own, with very good reason.

'Studying but not practising is to cheapen the teacher's transmission. But to practise without principles is to become sick from one's art.'

Many people, in the West particularly, 'study' Tai Chi Chuan, that is to say they read books, attend classes and ingest concepts, and go to endless workshops with different teachers to glean little gems of information. Tai Chi Chuan is a physical art and cannot be learned by study alone. It is a fallacy to think that because you have learned something intellectually that you are now competent to do it. Mostly this overly intellectual approach is due to misunderstanding, though sometimes it is simply laziness. There is a saying: 'Everybody wants to shine. Who wants to do the polishing?'

Conversely, to practise without studying and understanding the principles of Tai Chi Chuan will not develop the true art either. Correct practice and adherence to the principles is the only way to progress in Tai Chi Chuan. And only with constant correction, both against what you understand and by a competent teacher, can you acquire the true art.

Appendix IV – Supplementary Stretching Exercises

There follows a small collection of supplementary stretching exercises for the more advanced student who wishes to increase strength and flexibility, perhaps for martial arts purposes.

Cat Stretch: Place the feet one shoulder width apart with the hands two to two and a half shoulder widths in front of the feet, either with the palms, knuckles or fingers touching the floor (depending on the degree of difficulty required). Bring the body back then down so that your nose passes between your hands just above the floor. As your head comes forward and up, stretch up with your face, arching your back so that your hips brush the floor. Similar to a cat stretching.

Cat Stretch – starting position.

Cat Stretch – bring head back to begin forward swoop.

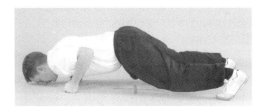

Cat Stretch – slide nose along, just above the floor.

Cat Stretch – arch the back and stretch up.

NB This is a strenuous exercise designed to flex and strengthen the back, arms shoulders and hips. Start slowly and do not attempt too many repetitions of the exercise until you become familiar with it. If you have a medical condition that may be affected by strenuous work, such as a heart condition or high blood pressure, consult your instructor and or physician before attempting this exercise.

Side Stretch Punch: Place your feet two to two and a half shoulder widths apart. Turn to the right and perform a reverse punch with the left fist, pulling back with the right elbow to maximize the twisting of the hips. Turn the body to the left so that you are in a horse stance and punch with

the right fist in the same direction that you previously punched with the left fist, this time pulling back with the left elbow. Turn back to the right and repeat the reverse punch with the left fist. (This is one set on one side of the body.) Turn to the left and continue turning until you can perform a reverse punch with the right fist 180 degrees from the direction of the previous punches. Turn back to the right and deliver a left punch in the direction of the previous punch, then turn back to the left and deliver another right reverse punch. Continue by repeating the first set, starting again from this position.

This exercise loosens the inner thighs, hips, lower back and spine and strengthens

Side Stretch Punch – starting position.

Side Stretch Punch – twist punch right.

Side Stretch Punch – straight punch right.

Side Stretch Punch – twist punch right.

Side Stretch Punch – twist punch left.

Side Stretch Punch – straight punch left.

Side Stretch Punch – twist punch left.

the shoulders and arms. It should be done fluidly and with the turning power of the body, rather than with the strength of the arms. Build up repetitions slowly starting with twenty and working up to one hundred.

Swing Stretch Punch: Place your feet two to two-and-a-half shoulder widths apart and make loose fists with your hands. Swing your right fist in a high arc in front of your body, turning the body to the left by pivoting on the soles of your feet, until your hips are 90 degrees from the line on which they started. Swing the right arm back in a high arc and follow it naturally with the left arm, rotating your body to the right until your hips face the opposite direction from their previous position. Continue to swing back and forth fluidly.

Swing Stretch Punch – leading left swing.

Swing Stretch Punch – following right swing.

Swing Stretch Punch – leading right swing about to begin.

FAR LEFT: Swing Stretch Punch – leading right swing.

Swing Stretch Punch – following left swing.

Hold Foot and Kick –
relax.

FAR RIGHT: Hold Foot
and Kick – stretch.

Swing Kick Stretch – swing out to right.

RIGHT: Swing Kick Stretch – swing across
to left.

This exercise loosens the upper back, shoulders and arms and strengthens the legs, hips, and lower back. Build up repetitions slowly starting with twenty and working up to one hundred.

Hold Foot and Kick: Stand straight up, breathe in and relax. Lift one knee till you can grasp the sole of the raised foot with both hands. Extend the raised foot, focusing on the heel and hold for a count of five as you breathe out. Breathe in and relax as you bring the foot back to the body. Repeat on the same side before switching legs.

This exercise is taken from a set of the Pa Tuan Jin. It is very useful for stretching the hamstrings, increasing balance and developing power in front kicks.

The Swing Kick Stretch: Stand straight up and extend your arms on either side of your body. Swing one foot up so that it connects with the hand on the same side of the body. Without pausing swing the foot down and up on the other side of the body so that it connects with the opposite hand. Continue to swing the foot from one side to the other starting with ten repetitions and working up to thirty repetitions. Repeat on the other leg.

This exercise increases flexibility in the inner thigh, hamstrings and hips and strengthens the legs and stomach muscles. It is also very good for improving the balance.

Twist Stretch: Stand with the feet two shoulder widths apart, breathe in and relax. Turn to the left as you breathe out, pivoting on the balls of the feet until the hips are 90 degrees from the position in which you started. Stretch up with the right hand and down with the left, keeping the back straight, so that you are looking at your left heel. Hold the position until you have expelled all the air from your lungs,

Twist Stretch – left.

Twist Stretch – right.

Hip Thrusts – arching back and thrusting hips.

Hip Thrusts – lowering back and thrusting buttocks.

then return to the starting position as you breathe in and relax. Repeat alternately eight times on each side.

This exercise is taken from a set of the Pa Tuan Jin. It is very useful for stretching and loosening the whole back and the hips.

Hip Thrusts: Rest on your hands and knees. Using your stomach and lower back muscles, thrust your hips forward as you arch your back (convex), breathing out. Hold the position for a count of three then thrust you buttocks back and make your back concave as you breathe in, again hold for a count of three. Repeat ten to thirty times. Alternatively thrust forward and back slowly and smoothly on a natural breath cycle.

This exercise provides gentle strengthening for the stomach and lower back muscles and increases flexibility in the lower back. It is also a useful aid to recovery if you have a weakness in the lower back.

Appendix V – Advice on Full-Contact Training and Equipment

There follows some advice for those who wish to engage in the practice of full-contact sparring. This form of training can be very dangerous and should only be undertaken with consent from your teacher and under properly controlled conditions. Engaging in such practice is always at the participant's own risk but every opportunity should be taken to minimize that risk!

Minimum Training Level and Physical Requirements

Before participating in full-contact training, it is recommended that combatants should be students at the Intermediate level, or above (that is, who have been training for three or more years, have covered all the basics and developed some skill in Push Hands and related exercises), have good break-falling skills, be physically fit and healthy, be at a similar level of training and ability and be within 28lb (12.5kg) in weight of each other.

Personnel

There should be a minimum of three assistants present, apart from the combatants. At least one of those assistants should be fully trained in first aid and recovery and one should have experience in controlling such bouts. One assistant should act as timekeeper using a suitable stopwatch.

Arena

As far as is practicable, the fighting area should be clearly defined, be free of obstacles and have a smooth unbroken surface.

Equipment – General

There should be a fully equipped first-aid box and a means of telephoning for help (mobile phone or land line). If the bout is to be held outside, there should be sufficient people and a stretcher available to carry an injured combatant to safety, should the need arise, and the training area should not be out of service of the mobile phone.

Equipment – Personal

The following items should be mandatory – full face head protector with impenetrable face plate, chest protector, groin protector, heavy mitts with wrist padding, shin protectors. Optional items may include: elbow protectors, knee protectors, forearm protectors, instep protectors and back protector.

Women should wear a purpose-made and well-fitting breast protector and not rely on a straightforward chest protector, such as would be worn by a man. Women should also use a groin protector; it is a common fallacy that a women's groin does not need protection in this kind of training.

NB Gumshields are not necessary when full face protection is used and should not be worn with full face headgear due to the danger of choking following a knockout, as it can take some time to remove headgear. Also, having to remove the headgear, because the combatant is choking on a gumshield, may endanger them if there is a possibility of spinal injury.

All equipment should be checked to ensure that it is in good condition at the start of the session and observed to remain so throughout. If a piece of equipment fails it should be replaced before the training continues and, if this is not possible, the training should be concluded. An example of typical full-contact safety equipment is shown opposite.

Combat view of full-contact equipment.

Front view of full contact equipment.

The Actual Bouts

The more tired you become the more likely it is that you will be injured. For this reason, bouts should be kept short with plenty of rest time between each one, for example, 1 or 2 minutes of actual fighting time followed by 1 to 5 minutes' rest, and the number of bouts should be kept low, perhaps only 2 or 3, unless the combatant's fitness level is very good. It is recommended that you continue to stand, or walk around in a relaxed manner, between bouts and that blankets are available to keep combatants warm if the area is cold. If you become too tired to continue call for a stop, don't be a hero.

To avoid confusion a clear set of pre-arranged signals should be agreed on before full-contact training is embarked upon and everyone involved should be fully conversant with them. It is usually best to stick to commands in your native language as they will be more readily absorbed and acted upon. A suggested system follows:

Only the person refereeing the bout should call GO, but anyone present, including the combatants, should be free to call STOP at any time if they feel it is important for the bout to be stopped for safety reasons, or the action has degenerated to the point where the combatants are brawling.

At a call of STOP, both combatants should stop immediately, stepping away from each other and keeping their guard up if possible (in case one combatant fails to hear the command to stop), the stopwatch should be stopped and only restarted when the referee calls GO. Before the bout is restarted the referee should be satisfied that both combatants are ready, that all equipment is intact, and that both combatants are fit to continue. When the time designated for the bout is up, the timekeeper should call STOP to end the bout.

Restrictions on Technique

Even with the use of protective equipment some techniques are too dangerous to be included in this type of training. The following techniques should not be used: striking to the throat or eyes, locking or throwing using the neck, attacking the joints with a kick, strike or other blow, biting (only possible if non full-face headgear is used) or grabbing the opponent's headgear. You may well decide to disallow other techniques as well but those mentioned should be considered an absolute no-no!

Following Up On a Successful Technique

Follow-up strikes to unprotected areas of the body (this may happen if a combatant turns away from, or is spun round by, an attack) should be done with minimum force. Locks or controlling techniques or throws that act against a joint should be done with restraint. If a combatant has been dropped or thrown to the floor the other combatant should follow up making only light contact to a protected area.

Other Safety Considerations

If a you are unwilling to continue with the bout your wishes should be respected and no person should try to persuade you to continue against your instincts.

If a combatant is knocked unconscious, no matter how brief the time, or exhibits any sign that they may be even partially concussed, the training should be concluded and the combatant should not undertake any further full-contact training for a minimum of six weeks. He or she should also visit a doctor at the earliest opportunity to ensure that no undetected injury has been sustained.

Etiquette

There is no place for anger or enmity in this sort of training and to ensure that everyone involved remains friends and that the discipline necessary for everyone's safety is adhered, to it is best to agree upon, and stick to, a formal protocol. Some suggestions of a typical and traditional nature follow:

Before the training commences both combatants should salute the referee, then each other.

During the training combatants should maintain the correct spirit and not allow themselves to become angered. If a combatant becomes angry, he or she should call STOP and not resume the training until or unless the anger has passed.

Combatants should accept the referee's decision without question during the training, and remain polite and respectful at all times. If you wish to question, or comment on, a decision, it should be done respectfully after the training has concluded. (It's a good idea to video such training, if at all possible, as it can increase the usefulness of such training to view the bouts later on.)

Combatants should strive to maintain self control at all times.

At the end of the last bout combatants should salute each other and then the referee.

Appendix VI – Self-Defence and British Law

The physical self-defence techniques shown in this book are dangerous. They must be practised with caution and only within the controlled environment of a supervised class. Many of the techniques can cause serious injury, prolonged or permanent disability, or death if applied in earnest during a confrontation with an assailant

The ramifications of applying martial arts techniques while defending yourself, your loved ones, or your property can be far reaching and potentially could result in you being charged with assault, manslaughter, or even murder.

The law regarding pleas of self-defence vary enormously from country to country: this book will only concern itself with the view of British law.

Under British law you need to be able to show two things clearly in order to succeed with a plea of self-defence:

1. That you truly believed you, or another person, were in immediate danger of being assaulted physically.
2. That you used only *reasonable force* to defend yourself.

Point one – immediate physical danger is much easier to prove if your attacker has initiated an attack. However, you cannot argue that you felt you were in immediate physical danger if someone assaults you but then backs off before you've had time to respond. The correct course of action in the eyes of the law is to bring a charge of assault against the attacker. If you retaliate and injure your attacker you cannot argue self-defence as you were engaged in an act of revenge.

Point two – using reasonable force is crucial to any argument of self-defence and is often hardest to prove. To give some examples: if you are confronted by an attacker armed with a knife it may be reasonable to pick up a piece of wood and possibly break your attacker's knife arm. If you carry on hitting him with the piece of wood after he has dropped the knife you may be charged with assault as you are no longer in such great physical danger. If you pick up a piece of wood to defend yourself from an unarmed attacker you will find it very hard to argue that you were using reasonable force, unless the attacker is *much* bigger than you and even then you will be on shaky ground.

On the other hand, if you carry any object *with the specific intention* of using it as a weapon of self-defence you are guilty of carrying an offensive weapon.

If an attacker is of similar, or slighter, build than yourself reasonable force is often viewed as: 'no more force than the attacker is trying to exert on you'. This is a very difficult situation. If you win, particularly against a punching and kicking attack, you will almost certainly have done more damage to your assailant than he did to you. Your best hope in this situation is that there are independent witnesses who will testify that you were attacked first and that you had no option but to fight back in the way you did.

At the end of the day what this all means is that claiming self-defence against a charge of assault relies on much subjective opinion on the part of jurors and the judiciary.

Think very carefully before committing yourself to physical violence, even in the name of self-defence. If you can give away your possessions, talk yourself out of it, walk away or run away (without leaving someone else in danger) you should do so.

You should follow the above advice even if you are a highly trained martial artist. In fact, especially if you are a highly trained martial artist! Judges and jurors tend to have the same misconceptions about the martial arts as the rest of society. They've all seen Kung Fu films or *Crouching Tiger, Hidden Dragon* and if they don't actually believe you can fly they will almost certainly think that you can defend yourself by flipping the attacker over with your fingers and placing them effortlessly in an

arm lock until the police arrive to cart them away, because you are a 'master' of the martial arts (even if you are in fact really a novice).

The 'bottom line' is: only ever use physical self-defence techniques when you have absolutely no other choice and, even then, be as restrained as you can given the circumstances. Moreover, never, ever continue to strike an assailant after he has stopped being a threat to you.

Lineage

The Lineage chart below is modelled on the chart used by my teacher, Master Lam Kam-Chuen. It does not show the Tung Bei, Boxing and Da Cheng Chuan strands, to which Master Lam is also entitled, as they are not directly related to the subject matter in this book.

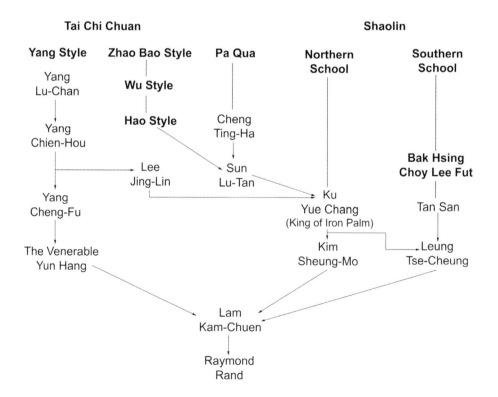

Index

Affirmation   63
Agility   92

Bag training   104–106
Body lightness   65
Breakfalls   16, 41, 73, 93, 109
Breathing   13, 17, 25, 55, 63, 94

Chan Ssu Jin   115–117
Change   11, 14, 24, 89, 91–93
Chen Sung Ching – the three firmnesses
    coordination   95
Chi (Qi)   13–14, 33, 49–50, 54–58, 94,
    121
Chi debate   49–50
Chi Kung (Qigong)   14–16, 22–23, 34,
    41, 121, 137
Chinese terms   12–15
Classics   29, 60, 89, 90, 94, 120, 121,
    128, 129, 141–147
Common questions   15
Confucianism   14
Constant rate   58
Continuity   58
Coordination   59–62
Correctness   24–28

Double Push Hands   69–72

Emperor Fist   101

Finding a teacher   19–21
Full contact sparring   154–157

Hero's Stroll   67–68
Hexagram   14, 89

Hsu Jing (finding the tiger amongst the
    corn)   124–125

I   121–122
I-Ching   14–15, 89, 123

Jin   13–14
Judo   16

Lao Tzu   14
Learning the form   24–32
Li   14, 60, 121–122
Ling Kong Jin   50

Making space   111–115
Meridian   14, 16, 22, 24–25, 33, 52,
    55–56, 94, 108

Nei Kung   14–16, 22–23, 34, 41, 49, 55,
    63–65, 121, 122, 137
Neutralizing   96, 117, 128–129, 144

Pa Qua   95
Pa Tuan Jin   136–141
Philosophy   89
Phoenix Eye   101
Push Hands   18, 20, 21, 54, 93–95,
    96–97, 120–127, 129

Redirection   109–111
Refinement of Jin into Shen   122–124
Relaxed force   68–69
Roundness   50–54

Self–defence   17, 42–45, 72–88
Sexual practice   58

Shen   60, 121, 122–123
Single Push Hands   35–41
Sinking   93–95, 108
Slowness (not hurrying)   29–30,
    62–63
Small Heavenly Circle   54, 56–58, 65
Spear Hand   101, 105
Sticking   35, 39, 108, 128, 129, 143,
    144
Stretching   17, 22, 24, 33, 34, 131–136
Sung   68, 93–95
Sung Jin   68–69, 104, 122

Tai Chi   12
Tai Chi Chuan   12
Tai Chi Kung   121
Tai Chi Sphere   120
Tai Chi wrestling   45
Tan Tien   13, 24, 52–58, 63–65, 68, 94,
    117, 120, 134, 136
Taoism   14
Technique sparring   99–100
Throwing   109–115

Ting Jin – listening to/sensitivity to force
    95–96, 125
Touch sparring   45–46
Trigram   89
Tung Jin – understanding force   124,
    125–126

Uprooting   18, 73, 79, 106, 109

Vital points   101, 103

Weapons   72, 123
Wu Chi   14, 124
Wushu   14, 19

Xing-I   95

Yielding   35, 39, 47, 96, 108, 125, 126,
    128, 129, 143, 144
Yin and Yang   9, 13, 14, 89, 119–120,
    121, 124

Zhan Zhuang   22, 33, 65